Individual Rights and Civic Responsibility

Civil Rights

David Seidman

The Rosen Publishing Group, Inc.
New York

To that groovy chick, Marilyn Papiewski, who digs that crazy Constitution the most.

Published in 2001 by The Rosen Publishing Group, Inc.
29 East 21st Street, New York, NY 10010

Library of Congress Cataloging-in-Publication Data

Seidman, David.
Civil rights / by David Seidman.
p. cm. — (Individual rights and civic responsibility)
Includes bibliographical references and index.
ISBN 0-8239-3231-1 (library binding)
1. Civil rights—United States—History—Juvenile literature.
2. Political rights—United States—History—Juvenile literature. [1. Civil rights. 2. Political rights.]
I. Title. II. Individual rights and civic responsibility.
KF4750 .S45 2001
323'.0973—dc21

2001000918

Manufactured in the United States of America

Contents

Introduction: How We Got Here

Democracy's a tough game. The people who rake in the most votes get to boss around the losers. But plenty of losers insist on getting the same rights as anyone else. They fight and sacrifice for their rights—and sometimes they pay for them in blood. The fight started long ago.

Around 1700 or 1800 BC, Hammurabi was king of Babylon, a Middle Eastern land that today is occupied mostly by Iraq. He created the Code of Hammurabi, the oldest surviving list of laws. "When Marduk [the god who ruled over humanity] sent me to rule over men," Hammurabi wrote at the start of the Code, "I did right . . . and brought about the well-being of the oppressed." At the end, he added that he wrote the Code "so that the strong might not injure the weak."

Hammurabi wasn't the only ancient force to demand fair treatment for the powerless. "You shall not wrong a stranger," reads the Bible's Book of Exodus, chapter 22, "[and] you shall not afflict any widow or fatherless child." The next chapter demands, "You shall not follow a multitude to do evil," a clear hint that the majority wasn't always right.

Centuries later, Jesus Christ felt the same way. As a Jew under Roman rule, he knew the feelings of an oppressed minority. He preached love, peace, mercy, and forgiveness; he spoke up for the poor and the weak. His example and teachings would lead many other people to fight for those who couldn't easily fight for themselves.

For most of human history, though, the people in charge didn't give anyone else much power or freedom. That was the case in the early 1200s, when the emotional, impulsive King John of England imposed high taxes, forced the people to follow arbitrary laws, and, in general, acted like a tyrant.

By 1215, England's noblemen, the barons, had had enough. They gave John a list of demands. In June he signed a version of the list, named the Magna Carta (Latin for Great Charter). "To no one will we sell, to no one will we refuse or delay, right or justice." "We decree and grant that all . . . cities, boroughs, towns, and ports shall have all their liberties and free customs." "We will and firmly order that . . . the men in our kingdom have and hold all the aforesaid liberties, rights, and concessions . . . in all respects and in all places, forever."

The Magna Carta didn't help just the barons. England had conquered the neighboring land of South Wales, and John promised to undo the harm that he and his troops had done to the Welsh. "If we have . . . removed Welshmen from lands or liberties, or other things . . . they shall be immediately

The Magna Carta was the first "bill of rights" for citizens. Here, King John signs the Magna Carta, surrounded by members of his court.

restored to them." He even guaranteed women a few rights ("No widow shall be compelled to marry, so long as she prefers to live without a husband"). The Magna Carta didn't help every group. It more or less banned all faiths except the Church of England, but it was a start.

The freedoms granted by the Magna Carta traveled across the ocean to the New World, America. In the early 1600s, English settlers landed in Virginia. Their charter guaranteed them the "liberties, franchises, and immunities" that people had "in our realm of England."

England wasn't the only nation to wrench history in new directions. More than 200 years later and 500 miles south, Portugal established the European trade in African slaves. Next door to Portugal, in Spain, King Ferdinand and Queen Isabella sent mariner Christopher Columbus on a voyage that found the Caribbean islands, southeast of Florida. Columbus eventually took some of the locals as slaves and started a trend that would last for centuries: trampling the rights of the people he called Indians.

In Holland, members of a Christian sect called the Pilgrims were unhappy. The Pilgrims wanted their own religion to be the established faith—that is, the official, government-sponsored religion, and the only one that people could follow legally. But Holland allowed a variety of religions, so the Pilgrims left. In 1620, they landed in Massachusetts, where they founded the Massachusetts Bay Colony as a Pilgrim stronghold. Then Roger Williams came along.

A non-Pilgrim minister who would eventually found the American Baptist church, Williams in 1633 insisted that the government not tell citizens what religion to practice. "Enforced uniformity . . . is the greatest occasion of

7

civil war, ravishing of conscience, persecution of Christ Jesus in his servants, and of the hypocrisy and destruction of millions of souls," he thundered in a document called "A Plea for Religious Liberty." "It is the will and command of God that . . . a permission of the most paganish, Jewish, Turkish, or anti-Christian consciences and worships be granted to all men."

The Pilgrim leaders threw Williams out. So he founded his own colony. He established the area that became the state of Rhode Island as a haven of religious tolerance.

Williams's expulsion may have made the Pilgrims think about such things as freedom and rights. In any event, the colonists created the Massachusetts Body of Liberties in 1641, to ensure "such liberties, immunities, and privileges as humanity, civility, and Christianity call for as due to every man." The document decreed the equality of all citizens: "Every person within this jurisdiction, whether inhabitant or foreigner, shall enjoy the same justice and law."

The Body of Liberties was no model of minority rights, however. It had little use for freedom of religion. "All the people of God within this jurisdiction . . . shall have full liberty to gather themselves into a church . . . provided they do it in a Christian way."

Still, the Body of Liberties set up America's first detailed list of rights and freedoms. By proposing that a government ensure equality for at least some citizens, it would inspire later documents.

Fast forward to 1775. The colonies were under English rule, and they hated it. Unlike Englishmen in England, the Englishmen in the colonies couldn't elect their own representatives to Parliament. English officials interfered with the colonists' commerce, took their property, and installed soldiers in their homes.

So the colonists shot them. In April 1775, when English soldiers marched on rebellious colonists, gunfire broke out. The Revolutionary War was on.

The fight for freedom uncorked the urge for all kinds of freedoms. In Virginia, local politician George Mason wrote the Virginia Bill of Rights. "All men are by nature equally free and independent, and have certain inherent rights . . . namely, the enjoyment of life and liberty, with the means of acquiring and possessing property, and pursuing and obtaining happiness and safety," the paper began. It became a model for the whole nation. But less than a month after Mason's document came an even more important one.

The Declaration of Independence, written by Thomas Jefferson, accused King George III of England of violating the colonists' rights. It also laid down a basic principle of American government. "We hold these truths to be self-evident, that all men are created equal, that they are endowed by their creator with certain unalienable rights, that among these are life, liberty, and the pursuit of happiness."

The United States was an independent country, and it needed a constitution. It got one: the Articles of Confederation. The Articles gave very little power to the federal government but plenty to the states.

As a result, the federal government was too weak to rule properly. The nation's leaders got together in Philadelphia during May 1787 to strengthen the government. Writing a whole new constitution wasn't part of their job.

They did it anyway. Primarily written by James Madison, a tiny (five foot four), young (he was thirty-six, compared to George Washington, who was fifty-five, and Benjamin Franklin, who was eighty-one) Virginia politician, the Constitution intended "to secure the blessings of liberty to ourselves and our posterity."

Article I decreed equality by outlawing English-style titles such as barons and kings: "No title of nobility shall be granted by the United States." Article VI discouraged discrimination by religion: "No religious test shall ever be required as a qualification to any office or public trust." And Article IV insisted that all American citizens had the same rights: "The citizens of each state shall be entitled to all privileges and immunities of citizens in the [other] states."

But the Constitution permitted slavery. It said not a word about the rights of women. It did virtually nothing for immigrants or Indians. It was mostly a diagram for a national government, not a guarantee of equal rights.

The delegates sent the Constitution to state legislatures and constitutional conventions for ratification. They probably didn't see what would come next.

Furious arguments broke out. To keep the central government from having too much power over their citizens, the states demanded that the Constitution include a list of the citizens' rights.

Madison offered a deal. He asked the states to approve the Constitution, on the condition that "the first Congress meeting under it ought to prepare and recommend to all states for ratification the most satisfactory provisions for all essential rights."

The offer worked. State after state ratified the Constitution. On March 4, 1789, the U.S. Congress met for the first time and built a list of amendments to the Constitution. On December 15, 1791, the states ratified ten of the amendments: the Bill of Rights.

Freedom of religion was included, as was a rule against cruel and unusual punishments for prisoners. There were protections to keep the government from exercising too much power: "No person shall be . . . deprived of life, liberty, and property without due process of law." The document even tried to make the power of the people and the state governments somewhat equal to the power of the federal government. "The powers not delegated to the United States by the Constitution . . . are reserved to the states respectively or to the people."

The amendments weren't perfect. The rights of women, African Americans, and other people would have to wait years for full protection.

Still, the Bill of Rights set up the basic freedoms that almost every American has wanted. The ways in which they've taken or lost those freedoms are the subject of the rest of this book.

1 African Americans

It's no secret that Europeans and Americans haven't always respected the rights of Africans. That's an understatement.

In the 1440s, for instance, slave traders began to steal people from West Africa to sell into slavery in Portugal. It was the beginning of a trade in slaves that would last for centuries. Clearly, the slave merchants weren't thinking about the rights of their "property"—other human beings.

Cut to the early 1510s and such Caribbean islands as Cuba and Hispaniola. They lie southeast of Florida and at the time were Spanish colonies. Spanish authorities faced a shortage of local people who wanted to work for them. The Spaniards imported Africans from the Guinea coast, near such modern nations as Nigeria and the Congo — the first known appearance of black slaves in the New World.

Slave trading came to American shores during 1619. In August, a Dutch ship delivered twenty Africans to Jamestown, Virginia.

Slavery spread through the colonies. By 1725, slaves numbered about 15 percent of the population—more than one person in every seven. In most colonies, a slave couldn't marry, get a jury trial, drink alcohol, learn to read, have a funeral, carry a weapon, or defend himself or herself against a white attacker. A slave's owner could work his slave as hard and long as he wanted and punish him or her any way he liked, including putting him or her to death (though some colonies did have laws against excessive cruelty).

Even though the American Revolution brought bold talk of rights and freedoms, slavery stayed in place. It was so important, especially in southern states, that it affected the creation of the U.S. Constitution. The Southern states wouldn't sign a document that abolished slavery or granted blacks the same rights as whites. The Southern states threatened to leave the union and break the infant nation into pieces.

So James Madison (a southern slaveholder himself) and the Constitution's other framers worked out a compromise. "The Constitution prohibited Congress from abolishing the African slave trade for two decades; [and] required states to return to their owners fugitives from bondage," writes historian Eric Foner in his book *The Story of American Freedom*. The nation stayed together.

When its citizens approved the Constitution on the condition that Congress add a bill of rights, they weren't thinking of rights for blacks. The ten amendments in the Bill of Rights never mentioned slavery, race, African Americans, or anything related to those topics.

So slavery went on. In 1790, Congress passed the Naturalization Act, which allowed only "free white persons" to become citizens. In Virginia, nearly half of the white families owned slaves. Overall, one-fifth of the nation lived in slavery.

Changes were in the air, though. Prominent politicians, including Benjamin Franklin and Virginia slaveholder Thomas Jefferson, had denounced slavery. Slaves spoke up for themselves, too. A 1777 petition from Massachusetts slaves to the state's House of Representatives read, "A great number of blacks detained in a state of slavery . . . have in common with all other men a natural and unalienable right to that freedom which the Great Parent of the Universe hath bestowed equally on all mankind."

In 1787, Congress' Northwest Ordinance forbade slavery in the Northwest Territory, which included Illinois, Indiana, Michigan, Ohio, and Wisconsin. By 1804, every northern state had passed laws abolishing slavery or gradually freeing the state's slaves. In 1808, Congress outlawed the trade in slaves from Africa, although whites could buy and sell slaves who were already in America, including the American-born children of slaves. In 1820, the Missouri Compromise allowed slavery in Missouri and Oklahoma but outlawed it in Iowa, Minnesota, Kansas, and Nebraska.

A public antislavery movement began to rise. In 1831, the passionate, twenty-five-year-old white Massachusetts abolitionist William Lloyd Garrison started publishing the *Liberator*, an antislavery magazine.

Garrison was politically passionate. He publicly burned a copy of the Constitution because it tolerated slavery. Declaring "no union with slaveholders," he demanded the "immediate dissolution" of the United States. In the *Liberator's* first issue, he wrote, "I will not equivocate—I will not excuse—I will not retreat a single inch — and *I will be heard.*"

He was. The *Liberator*, along with the American Anti-Slavery Society that Garrison helped to organize, inflamed the small but growing number of people who opposed slavery.

But the slaveholders weren't going quietly. In 1854 Congress passed the controversial Kansas-Nebraska Act, which allowed citizens of those territories to decide for themselves if they wanted to be slave states.

The Kansas-Nebraska Act wasn't the only law to aid slavery. From 1793 onward, Congress had been passing Fugitive Slave Laws to strengthen the Constitution's Article IV, Section 3: "No person held to service or labor in one state, under the laws thereof, escaping into another, shall . . . be discharged from such service or labor, but shall be delivered [back to his or her owner]."

In 1836, Missouri surgeon John Emerson brought his slave, Dred Scott, to Illinois and Minnesota, and took him back to Missouri two years later. After Emerson died in 1846, Scott sued Emerson's widow for freedom. Because slavery was illegal in Illinois and Minnesota, Scott claimed that living there had freed him. Mrs. Emerson transferred Scott's ownership to her brother, John Sandford, who fought the case.

In 1857, *Dred Scott v. Sandford* reached the U.S. Supreme Court, which turned down Scott. The Court's chief justice, Roger Taney, wrote that African Americans were "a subordinate and inferior class of human beings" who "had no rights which the white man was bound to respect." The Dred Scott decision infuriated abolitionists, tore up political parties, and led to the Civil War (1861–1865).

The war brought freedom for slaves. The Emancipation Proclamation of January 1, 1863, freed thousands. The Thirteenth Amendment (ratified on December 6, 1865) settled the matter completely. "Neither slavery nor involuntary servitude, except as a punishment for crime whereof the party shall have been duly convicted, shall exist within the United States."

But freedom didn't mean equality. White Americans in both the North and the South discriminated against African Americans. In particular, they blocked blacks from voting.

What's more, southern states passed the Black Codes, which were laws that didn't allow African Americans to travel, own property, testify in court, or gather in unsupervised meetings. The Black Codes also inflicted harsher punishments on black criminals than on white ones. Public places eventually sprouted "white" and "colored" sections, and it was illegal for African Americans to use "white" facilities.

The Fourteenth Amendment (1868) should have ended the Black Codes. "All persons born or naturalized in the United States are citizens of the United States," the amendment said. "No state shall make or enforce any law which shall abridge the privileges or immunities of citizens of the United States; nor shall any state deprive any person of life, liberty, or property without due process of law; nor deny to any person within its jurisdiction the equal protection of the laws."

In 1892, shoemaker Homer Plessy—a man seven-eighths white and one-eighth black—tested the amendment. By Louisiana law, Plessy was black. The state's Separate Car Act demanded separate train cars for whites and blacks. But Plessy sat in a "white" car on the East Louisiana Railroad.

After he was ordered to sit in the "colored" section, Plessy sued, saying that the Separate Car Act violated the Fourteenth Amendment. The judge, John Howard Ferguson, ruled against him.

Plessy took his case—now called *Plessy v. Ferguson*—to the U.S. Supreme Court in 1896. He lost. As Justice Henry Brown wrote, the Fourteenth Amendment "could not have been intended to abolish distinctions based upon color, or to enforce social [equality], as distinguished from political equality, or a commingling of the two races."

The government wouldn't help African Americans, so they decided to help themselves. A group of black and white progressives formed the National Association for the Advancement of Colored People (NAACP) in 1909. The Urban League, a group with similar goals, was born in 1910. Around the same time, hundreds of thousands of blacks migrated from the South to the North, where racism was not so openly brutal.

Eventually, the government responded. In 1937's *West Coast Hotel Company v. Parrish*, the Supreme Court ruled that no business could violate a citizen's legal rights. In 1938's *United States v. Carolene Products*, the Court warned that it would closely examine laws "directed at particular religious or national or racial minorities" and "prejudice against discrete and insular minorities."

The next year, Attorney General Frank Murphy set up the Department of Justice's first Civil Liberties Unit to fight violations of civil rights. In 1941, President Franklin

African Americans have been fighting for equality for decades. This image of civil rights workers in an NAACP office dates from the 1940s.

Roosevelt set up the Fair Employment Practices Commission to investigate racism in hiring. In 1944, the U.S. Supreme Court told southern states to stop holding all-white elections.

Racism continued, though. Whites lynched blacks— they hanged them for alleged crimes without a trial or for no crime at all. In 1943, thousands of Detroit auto workers went on a "hate strike" against black employees. In many places, particularly the south, white officials blocked blacks from voting by charging high "poll taxes" to vote, making blacks prove they could read and write exceptionally well, evicting them from their homes, firing them from their jobs, and beating them bloody. Most segments of American society remained segregated, including the armed forces.

President Harry Truman was a grandson of slaveholders and in private called African Americans derogatory names, but the feisty Missourian also believed in equal rights. In 1948, he asked Congress to outlaw lynching, protect the right to vote, end "separate but equal" policies in transportation between states, and strengthen the civil rights laws that were already on the books. He also integrated the armed forces. That same year, the Supreme Court outlawed segregation in some housing contracts.

That ruling was just an appetizer. Six years later, the Court handed down a feast: *Brown v. Board of Education of Topeka, Kansas.*

Topeka had "separate but equal" schools. Black third-grader Linda Brown lived only a few blocks from a white school but had to attend a "colored" school, which meant walking a mile and passing through an unsafe railway switchyard. Oliver Brown, Linda's father, tried to enroll her in the white school, but the principal said no. So did Topeka's board of education. With the help of the NAACP, Oliver Brown sued.

On May 17, 1954, Chief Justice Earl Warren announced, "In the field of public education, the doctrine of 'separate but equal' has no place. Separate educational facilities are inherently unequal. Therefore, we hold that the plaintiffs . . . [have been] deprived of the equal protection of the laws guaranteed by the 14th Amendment."

In public schools at least, the Court had overturned *Plessy v. Ferguson*. The fight was on to desegregate all aspects of American society.

In 1955, forty-three-year-old black seamstress and activist Rosa Parks of Montgomery, Alabama, broke a local law: She refused to give up her seat on a bus to a white rider. The police arrested her. Montgomery's black community, including the rising young minister Dr. Martin Luther King Jr., began depriving the bus system of money by refusing to ride the buses. The boycott took more than a year, but it eventually got the buses desegregated.

Over the furious objections of southerners, Congress passed the Civil Rights Act of 1957. The act set up the Commission on Civil Rights to investigate inequality and set up a Civil Rights Division in the Justice Department to enforce civil rights laws.

In September 1957, Governor Orval Faubus of Arkansas ordered the National Guard to block nine black students from entering the city of Little Rock's all-white Central High School. It took four weeks of arguments and

1,000 paratroopers called out by President Dwight Eisenhower to get the teenagers into school.

In 1960, workers at a lunch counter in a Woolworth's department store in Greensboro, North Carolina, refused to serve four black college students. Each day the students sat at the counter, waiting to be served. The Greensboro sit-in lasted for nearly six months, and ended with the black customers getting the service that they'd wanted all along.

News of the sit-in spread. Other activists copied it. In 1960 alone, more than 50,000 people joined sit-ins, marches, and other civil-rights demonstrations. In 1961, the civil-rights group CORE (Congress of Racial Equality) sent hundreds of volunteers—"freedom riders"—on bus trips to see whether blacks and whites would be allowed to sit together. Angry mobs attacked them.

Mobs weren't the only danger. During a single week in 1963, "over 15,000 Americans were arrested in 186 cities [for opposing racist laws]," wrote Eric Foner. One of the most scandalous events took place in Birmingham, Alabama. White police attacked peaceful civil-rights demonstrators with dogs and high-pressure blasts from fire hoses, and then flung them into prison.

President John Kennedy told a national television audience that he would send Congress a bill to fix the situation. When it became law a year later, the Civil Rights Act of 1964 turned out to be what was possibly the most important statute on equality in nearly a century.

The act outlawed or heavily discouraged racial discrimination in voting, housing, education, employment, public places (such as hotels and restaurants), and other areas. It permitted the attorney general to sue anyone who violated the law, strengthened the Commission on Civil Rights, and created the federal Equal Opportunity Commission to make sure employers chose workers fairly.

Two additional laws nailed down the right to vote. The Twenty-Fourth Amendment, ratified in 1964, outlawed poll taxes in national elections. (Two years later, the Supreme Court outlawed state and local poll taxes). In 1965, President Lyndon Johnson proposed the Voting Rights Act, which abolished many literacy tests and other roadblocks.

Progress kept marching. The Civil Rights Act of 1968 fought discrimination in housing. The next year, the Supreme Court ordered school districts that were dragging their feet on integration to finish the job "at once." In 1970, Congress outlawed all literacy tests for voting. In 1971, the Supreme Court in *Griggs v. Duke Power Company* forced companies with a small number of minority employees to explain why they had so few. By the end of the year, employers who wanted to do business with the federal government had to set up goals and schedules for hiring minorities.

During the 1970s, the struggle for civil rights slowed. There were simply fewer major battles to fight. Besides, the country was growing more conservative and was, perhaps, less willing to shatter its old institutions.

The new era's most controversial equality-related issue was preferential treatment for minorities, also called affirmative action. The idea dated from more than a century earlier. In 1867, Congressman Thaddeus Stevens proposed that the government should give each ex-slave forty acres and a mule

Eng.ᵈ by A.H.Ritchie.

Frederick Douglass was one of the foremost leaders of the abolitionist movement. He served as an adviser to President Abraham Lincoln during the Civil War and fought for the adoption of amendments that guaranteed rights for blacks.

to set up as an independent farmer. The distinguished writer, lecturer, and ex-slave Frederick Douglass agreed. "When we consider the long years of slavery, the years of enforced ignorance, the years of injustice, of cruel strifes and degradation to which the Negro was doomed, the duty of the nation is not, and cannot be, performed by simply letting him alone," he said in 1894.

Seventy-one years later, President Lyndon Johnson spoke the same way. "You do not wipe away the scars of centuries by [merely] saying, 'Now you are free to go where you want.' You do not take a person who for years has been hobbled by chains and liberate him, bring him to the starting line and say, 'You are free to compete with all the others.'" In 1964, the Rev. Dr. Martin Luther King Jr. said that since "our society has been doing something special against the Negro for hundreds of years," the country should "do something special *for* him now."

The Supreme Court took on the issue in 1978's *Regents of the University of California v. Bakke*. In 1973, the university had turned down Allan Bakke's application to medical school. Bakke said the university excluded him for being white, because it had set up affirmative-action quotas to increase the percentage of nonwhite students. Bakke won the case, but the Court continued to permit racial preferences.

Other parts of the government had different views. In President Ronald Reagan's executive branch, Assistant Attorney General William Bradford Reynolds told Congress in 1981, "We will no longer insist upon or in any respect support the use of numerical or statistical formulas

"I Have a Dream"

In August 1963, the Rev. Dr. Martin Luther King Jr. spoke in Washington, DC to 250,000 people—one of the largest crowds that had ever gathered in the United States' capital. He delivered one of the greatest speeches in history.

"I have a dream that one day on the red hills of Georgia, sons of former slaves and sons of former slave-owners will be able to sit down together at the table of brotherhood.

"I have a dream that one day, even the state of Mississippi, a state sweltering with the heat of injustice, sweltering with the heat of oppression, will be transformed into an oasis of freedom and justice.

"I have a dream my four little children will one day live in a nation where they will not be judged by the color of their skin but by the content of their character . . .

"Let freedom ring from the mighty mountains of New York. Let freedom ring from the heightening Alleghenies of Pennsylvania. Let freedom ring from the snow-capped Rockies of Colorado . . .

"And when we allow freedom to ring, when we let it ring from every village and hamlet, from every state and city, we will be able to speed up that day when all of God's children—black men and white men, Jews and Gentiles, Catholics and Protestants—will be able to join hands and to sing in the words of the old Negro spiritual, 'Free at last, free at last; thank God Almighty, we are free at last.' "

25

designed to provide non-victims of discrimination preferential treatment based upon race."

In the 1990s, President Bill Clinton weighed in by saying of affirmative action, "Mend it, don't end it." In 1995's *Adarand Constructors, Inc. v. Pena*, the Supreme Court ruled that federal programs couldn't use racial preferences except to repair specific examples of discrimination. Simply being a member of a minority group wasn't enough to earn special treatment.

Moreover, according to the Associated Press, civil-rights crimes were the Justice Department's lowest priority between 1992 and 1996. The department prosecuted only 4 percent of the civil rights complaints that citizens filed in that time.

The citizens just filed more. The department said that the number of complaints more than doubled from 1990 to 1999. In 1998 alone, Americans filed more than 42,000 complaints. The largest segment was employment-discrimination cases.

Racism on the job isn't the only issue to infuriate African Americans. In recent years and to the present day, black leaders have been complaining about the shortage of black people on television and in other media. Some have also been demanding that the government offer payments to the descendants of slaves.

The biggest recent issue is a matter of life and death. Shootings and beatings of African Americans in New York City, Los Angeles, New Orleans, Cincinnati, and other communities have shone a light on racism in police departments. Many an African American driver has been stopped by cops for simply "driving while black." This is called racial profiling.

President Reagan's Assistant Attorney General William Bradford Reynolds told Congress in 1981, "We will no longer insist upon or in any respect support the use of numerical or statistical formulas designed to provide non-victims of discrimination preferential treatment based upon race."

No one can predict the next big controversy dealing with the rights of African Americans. But one thing seems sure. The issue won't vanish for a long time.

2 Women

"Neither earth nor ocean produces a creature as savage and monstrous as woman."
—Euripides, Greek dramatist, circa 425 BC

"Nature intended women to be our slaves . . . Women are nothing but machines for producing children."
—Napoleon Bonaparte, French emperor, circa 1800s

"Direct thought is not an attribute of femininity. In this, woman is now centuries . . . behind man."
—Thomas Edison, American inventor, 1912

With some of history's most brilliant men spouting attitudes like those, no wonder women have had a hard fight for equal rights.

It's actually been quite an up-and-down ride. Although many ancient cultures treated women as virtual slaves,

Babylon's Code of Hammurabi gave women some control over property, including businesses. They also had an equal say in raising their children.

However, the Greek philosopher Aristotle described women as inferior versions of men, and his teachings influenced Western culture for centuries. The early days of Christianity had a few elements of equality for women but many limits on their freedom.

The mixture of rights and restrictions (mostly restrictions) continued. Britain's Magna Carta gave women some respect, providing, "No widow shall be compelled to marry, so long as she prefers to live without a husband." At the same time, some of the articles in the document didn't show trust in women. "No one shall be arrested or imprisoned upon the appeal of a woman for [causing] the death of any[one] other than her husband."

This was the tradition that European settlers brought to America. Luckily, women had an advantage: men outnumbered them by as much as 200 to 1.

Usually, a tiny minority is a weak minority. But the imbalance was so lopsided that it made women valuable. In the early 1600s, the settlement of Jamestown, Virginia, "offered women free land, attractive to individuals who could otherwise never own land," explains historian Christine Lunardini in her book *Women's Rights*. Massachusetts' Body of Liberties decreed, "Every married woman shall be free from bodily correction or stripes [welts caused by whipping] by her husband, unless it be in his own defense upon her assault." Maryland had the colonies' first female lawyer and all-woman jury.

Mostly, though, women were short on rights. English law stated that after marriage, "the very being or legal existence of the woman is suspended." According to a practice called coverture, a woman's property and income belonged to her husband. Society discouraged women from entering careers outside of housework and child rearing. They could not vote, sign contracts, or file lawsuits. Up to one-half of colonial women—as many as three-quarters in some areas—weren't taught to read.

Even after seceding from England, the new United States didn't give women equality. The Declaration of Independence put it plainly: "All men are created equal." There were no female delegates to the convention that drafted the Constitution. The resulting document doesn't mention women at all.

It doesn't mention men, for that matter. It mentions people or persons, and so it provided at least the potential for equal rights. The only place where the Constitution mentions gender is in describing the president ("He shall hold his office during the term of four years," for instance).

The Bill of Rights includes a bit more. No citizen, states the Fifth Amendment, "shall be compelled in any criminal case to be a witness against himself." The Sixth Amendment states that a person accused of a crime has the right "to be confronted with the witnesses against him; [and] to have compulsory process for obtaining witnesses in his favor."

That's all though. Because writers often used "he" to stand for "he or she," and "him" for "him or her," the Constitution and the Bill of Rights are fairly gender-blind. In fact, no amendment specified gender until the Fourteenth Amendment in 1868 ("when the right to vote . . . is denied to any of the male inhabitants of [a] state . . . the basis of representation therein shall be reduced in the proportion which the number of such male citizens shall bear to the whole number of male citizens").

In any event, most if not all of the men who ran the government and businesses simply didn't think about women's rights. Women did, though. Wage-earning women wanted the same rights as working men. Women of property argued that since they paid taxes, they deserved the same rights as tax-paying men, including the right to vote. Starting with New York's Troy Female Seminary in 1821, educators began opening colleges that admitted women. "Women frequently attend public meetings," said French observer Alexis de Toqueville in his 1831 landmark book, *Democracy in America*, "and listen to political harangues as a recreation from their household labors."

Even more important was a wave of religious revivals that rolled across the first half of the 1800s. According to historian Richard Shenkman, author of *Legends, Lies, and Cherished Myths of American History*, America's population grew from four million in 1780 to 31 million in 1860 (a nearly eightfold increase), but the number of congregations grew from 2,500 to 52,000 (an increase of twentyfold).

The newly religious, both men and women, opposed a variety of immoral activities. The antislavery movement in particular often allowed women to participate with speeches and other activities, but not always.

In 1840, the World Anti-Slavery Conference, held in England, wouldn't let women onto the convention floor or the podium where the leaders were running things. Women had to sit in the balcony as spectators, not participants.

Lucretia Mott was a women's rights advocate and was also active in the Underground Railroad, which helped African Americans escape slavery.

One of those women was Lucretia Mott, a devout Quaker and antislavery organizer. Another was an admirer of Mott's, a woman nearly half her age, a passionate, fiery, twenty-four-year-old newlywed named Elizabeth Cady Stanton. Mott, Stanton, and other women didn't like being shoved aside. Their resentment came to a boil in 1848.

In the quiet, lakeside town of Seneca Falls in upstate New York, where Stanton lived with her husband and children, she and Mott and three other women met during early July to call for America's first Women's Rights Convention. A few days later, 240 women and forty men gathered in a Seneca Falls Methodist Church.

Stanton wrote the meeting's main proclamation. The Declaration of Sentiments closely followed the Declaration of Independence in form (a list of complaints) and style. "We hold these truths to be self-evident, that all men and women are created equal," read the Declaration. "Because women do feel themselves aggrieved, oppressed, and fraudulently deprived of their most sacred rights, we insist that they have immediate admission to all the rights and privileges which belong to them as citizens of the United States."

Following the Seneca Falls example, women's rights meetings began to pop up in state after state and got things done. By the end of 1887, nearly every state had given women the right to control their own income.

However women didn't have the right to vote, known as suffrage. In 1867, Kansas became the first state to hold a referendum on the issue. The voters (all male, of course) rejected it. To fight for the vote, Elizabeth Cady Stanton and her close colleague Susan Brownell Anthony formed the National Woman Suffrage Association (NWSA) in 1869.

Victory took a long time. Around 1872, NWSA member Virginia Minor of St. Louis, Missouri, sued local registrar of voters Reese Happersett for refusing to let her register to vote. When *Minor v. Happersett* reached the U.S. Supreme Court in 1874, the justices unanimously voted against her.

The legislative branch, too, opposed suffrage. In 1868 Kansas Senator S. C. Pomeroy introduced the first national woman's suffrage bill; it ultimately failed. In 1878 California Senator A. A. Sargent proposed a constitutional amendment, written by Susan B. Anthony, to grant women the vote. The Senate crushed the amendment, but senators would re-introduce it in every session over the next four decades.

Meanwhile, the NWSA—soon renamed the National American Woman Suffrage Association, or NAWSA—kept pushing. From 1869 to 1912, nine states and territories gave women the vote. Activists like the militant Alice Paul kept the heat on, picketing the White House for weeks on end (she even chained herself to the White House fence).

When policemen violently attacked the women, the cause gained public sympathy. What's more, Americans could see that the states that had given women the vote were carrying on business and government quite nicely, and that women responsibly took care of themselves, their families, and some businesses while men fought in World War I (1914–1918).

In August 1920, Anthony's amendment became the law: "The right of citizens of the United States to vote shall not be denied or abridged by the United States or by any states on account of sex. Congress shall have the power to enforce this article by appropriate legislation."

Susan B. Anthony

When Susan B. Anthony and eight other women tried to cast ballots in 1872's presidential election, the police arrested them. Anthony stood up in court and fought back, declaring that to women "This government is not a democracy. It is not a republic. It is an odious aristocracy; a hateful oligarchy of sex: the most hateful aristocracy ever established on the face of the globe." The judge convicted her of civil disobedience.

Flush with success, Alice Paul proposed the Equal Rights Amendment: "Men and women shall have equal rights throughout the United States and every place subject to its jurisdiction. Congress shall have the power to enforce this article by appropriate legislation." Congress turned it down.

It was the start of a new set of doldrums. Individual women scored great achievements, but the fight for equal rights subsided.

Things even went backward. The Supreme Court, in 1923's *Muller v. Oregon*, overturned an existing minimum-wage law for women. In 1929, Congress repealed 1921's Sheppard-Tower Act, which meant to improve health care for mothers and pregnant women, among others. During the 1930s, "many states and localities prohibited the hiring of women whose husbands earned a 'living wage,' and employers from banks to public school systems adopted rules barring married women from jobs," writes historian Eric Foner.

World War II (1939-1945) changed the situation. When the war drafted men out of the civilian workforce and into the military, women filled a wide variety of jobs that were restricted previously to men. In many cases, they also received equal pay.

When the war ended, though, women's rights returned to their prewar status. Things stayed that way for years.

In 1963, things began to change. Congress passed the Equal Pay Act, which California representative Helen Gahagan Douglas had first proposed in the 1940s. "No employer," stated the act, "shall discriminate . . . between employees on the basis of sex by paying wages to employees . . . at a rate less than the rate at which he pays wages to employees of the opposite sex . . . for equal work."

Possibly more important was *The Feminine Mystique*, a book by journalist and homemaker Betty Friedan. The feminine mystique was the idea that women should concern themselves primarily with housework, childcare, prettiness, and, above all, pleasing men. Friedan called the mystique a trap full of poisonous lies, and her book touched off a new movement, eventually called women's liberation.

More help came from a man whose politics were very different from those of hot-tempered, liberal Friedan. Virginia Representative Howard W. Smith opposed the new Civil Rights Act that was working its way through Congress. The act was meant to help African Americans get equal rights. Smith felt that it would elevate blacks over white women. With the help of other congressmen who hated African American rights, plus five congresswomen, Smith got Congress to make the Act's Title VII enforce gender equality on the job. "It shall be an unlawful employment practice . . . to discriminate against any individual . . . because of such individual's race, color, religion [or] sex."

Title VII wasn't enough. Betty Friedan and colleagues such as University of Wisconsin professor Kay Clarenbach got together on June 29, 1966, at the Washington, DC, Hilton Hotel to start their own group: the National Organization for Women.

NOW was a political force, fighting "to take the actions needed to bring women into the mainstream of American society, now, [with] full equality for women, in fully equal partnership with men" (as its first declaration announced). The group led demonstrations and marches, proposed legislation, and became what was possibly the most famous name in women's rights.

Women earned victory after victory. Take the year 1972, for instance. Chief of Naval Operations Elmo Zumwalt forbade sexism in the navy, reversing long-standing policies that stopped women from seagoing duty. Congress passed the Educational Amendments Act; its Title IX outlawed gender discrimination in educational activities and programs that receive federal funds. Congress also passed the Equal Rights Amendment, which read, "Equality of rights under the law shall not be denied or abridged by the United States or by any state on account of sex." The ERA would become a Constitutional amendment if thirty-eight states ratified it by July 1, 1982. By the end of 1972, more than twenty states ratified it.

In the end, though, only thirty-five states ratified the bill. The ERA died, largely because of opposition from conservative women, such as outspoken St. Louis, Missouri, lawyer and mother of six Phyllis Schlafly. The amendment, she said, would "deprive the American woman of many of the fundamental special privileges we now enjoy."

After the defeat of the ERA, the fight for women's rights shriveled. Still, some issues continued strong. The biggest was abortion.

Texas had outlawed the procedure. A woman named Roe (not her real name, but one that the legal system gave her to protect her privacy) decided to have an abortion and fight the law. In *Roe v. Wade* (1973), the U.S. Supreme Court decided that a woman's decision about whether or not to have a baby was her own private business. Abortion was officially a legal right.

Five years later, the 1978 case *Regents of the University of California v. Bakke* got into another area that affected women. It permitted affirmative action in hiring and other areas to make matters fair and equal for groups that had suffered discrimination, including women.

Another crucial issue was sexual harassment. Sexual advances, comments, and threats can make any job a nightmare. The Supreme Court outlawed such behavior in 1986, but the issue got its biggest headlines in September 1991. Law professor Anita Hill told the Senate Judiciary Committee that her former boss, Supreme Court nominee Clarence Thomas, had made her suffer horribly by pressuring her to date him, talking to her about his genitals, and describing obscene movies to her. The Senate confirmed Thomas's nomination, but the issue of sexual harassment has remained powerful.

Today, leaders of the women's rights movement point out that for all of their strides women don't always get equal rights. They often earn less than men for the same work. Violence against women is a hot issue, too—especially after the Supreme Court in 2000 struck down the Violence Against Women Act of 1994, a law allowing rape victims to sue rapists.

Perhaps the biggest trend is the rise of women's rights internationally. In October 2000, thousands of women from more than thirty countries marched on Washington, DC, to draw the government's attention to women's rights around the world.

That was not the only demonstration. In April 2000, six thousand women from all over the world came to Baltimore for Feminist Expo 2000. The conference tackled issues such as women's rights under the Taliban in Afghanistan, the abortion drug RU-486, and an international document called the Convention to Eliminate All Forms of Discrimination Against Women.

Whether this meeting will simply pass forgotten into history or turn out to have been as crucial as the Seneca Falls convention is still not known. But Expo speaker Gloria Steinem, a feminist in the 1960s, may have been right when she declared, "Don't let [our opponents] impede the movement by calling it over. We are thirty years into a century of change."

3 Native Americans

First class, first rate, first come, first served—to be first is to get the best treatment.

This wasn't true for the first Americans. Call them Indians or Native Americans, but the first people in America didn't get full rights.

The problem started in 1492, when Christopher Columbus reached the Caribbean island Hispaniola. He thought he was in or near India, so he called the locals Indians. Columbus and other voyagers from Spain enslaved the Indians and killed them if they resisted.

About a century passed before North America's Indians met many European settlers. After landing in Virginia in 1607 and Massachusetts in 1620, colonists from England and Holland got along with the Native Americans at first.

By the 1640s, the colonists were taking the Natives' land and forcing them to become Christians. Not every colonist favored this treatment—Roger Williams, founder of Rhode Island, protested vigorously—but it continued nonetheless.

Naturally, the Indians didn't like it. By 1700, they were fighting wars against English colonists on the Atlantic coast and Spaniards who were settling the Southwest.

Once the United States declared itself independent, the young country quickly made rules for dealing with native tribes. The first set of national governing laws, 1781's Articles of Confederation, handed great powers to the state governments and very few powers to the federal government. But Native American affairs were so important that the Articles gave Congress "the sole and exclusive rights and power of . . . regulating the trade and managing all affairs with the Indians."

When the Constitution (1789) replaced the Articles of Confederation, it stated much the same thing: "The Congress shall have power . . . to regulate commerce . . . with the Indian tribes." In 1790, the first of several Trade and Intercourse Acts ordered Americans to get the federal government's permission before making trade deals with the Native Americans.

For a while, the government seemed to respect the Indians. The most basic statement was probably the Northwest Ordinance (1787). "The utmost good faith shall always be observed toward the Indians; their lands and property shall never be taken from them without their consent; and in their property, rights, and liberty, they shall never be invaded or disturbed."

Still, there were some ominous signs. The federal government placed Indian matters under the Department of War (today called the Department of Defense).

In 1803, Thomas Jefferson was the president. He had recently made the Louisiana Purchase, a deal to buy a huge swath of western land. He proposed that the government move Indians in the eastern part of the country from their own land into the newly bought western territories, whether they wanted to go or not. Usually smaller than the lands that they'd given up, the spaces reserved for Indians were naturally called reservations. Over the next several decades, removal became a standard way that the government dealt with the native peoples.

The Indians fought for their rights. Big battles and small wars killed both Indians and whites. Overall, though, the Indians usually lost.

They lost in court, too. In the 1823 case *Johnson & Graham's Lessee v. McIntosh*, the first Supreme Court case to deal with Indian land, the Court limited the Indians' ability to sell the land. They could sell it to the U.S. government, and to anyone whom the government approved, but not to anyone else.

Enforcing such rules took a strong organization. On June 30, 1824, President James Monroe and Secretary of War John C. Calhoun created the Bureau of Indian Affairs, a formal, structured center of power within the War Department. The bureau eventually came to dominate Indian schools, courts, police, treaties, trade, and nearly everything else concerning the Indians.

Monroe was weak compared to Andrew Jackson, who became president in 1829. A rough-and-tumble backwoodsman who didn't care much about treaties, rights, or other niceties, Jackson led troops against indigenous peoples during the Creek Indian War (1813–1814) and forced the Creeks to surrender millions of acres of their lands. A few years later, Jackson killed masses of Indians in the First Seminole War (1817–1819) and became military governor of the Seminole lands.

Then he became president. "We now propose to acquire the countries occupied by the red men of the South and West by a fair exchange, and, at the expense of the United States, to send them to a land where their existence may be prolonged," he told Congress on December 6, 1830. To carry out his plan, Congress passed the Indian Removal Act of 1830.

The act may have encouraged states to make their own moves against the Indians. The Cherokee had long lived under their own laws in what had become the state of Georgia. The state and county governments decided to seize the land and "extend all the laws of Georgia over the same [land]; to abolish the Cherokee laws; and to deprive the Cherokees of the protection of their laws," the Supreme Court explained.

The Cherokees sued. In 1831's *Cherokee Nation v. Georgia*, the Court had to decide (as Chief Justice John Marshall put it), "Is the Cherokee nation a foreign state?"

The court's decision was: Yes and no. "[Native tribes] may more correctly, perhaps, be denominated domestic dependent nations," Marshall said. "Their relation to the United States resembles that of a ward to his guardian."

What exactly did that statement mean?

In 1829, Congregational minister Samuel Worcester of Vermont entered Georgia's Cherokee territory. The state government ordered him to swear that he'd support and obey the state's laws.

Worcester said no. He insisted that when he was on Cherokee land, he was under Cherokee law, not under the laws of Georgia.

The state sentenced Worcester to prison for four years at hard labor, but the case didn't end there. Worcester pushed it to the Supreme Court.

"The forcible seizure and abduction of [Worcester], who was residing in the [Cherokee] nation with its permission . . . is void, as being repugnant to the constitution, treaties, and laws of the United States," Marshall wrote in *Worcester v. Georgia* (1832). "The Cherokee nation . . . is a distinct community occupying its own territory, with boundaries accurately described, in which the laws of Georgia can have no force."

"John Marshall has made his decision," said President Jackson. "Now, let him enforce it." Marshall, of course, could do no such thing. The president's branch of government enforces the Court's decisions, if the president tells it to do so. The Court could say that the Indian tribes were nations, herds, or the Kingdom of Heaven, but Jackson and later presidents treated them like prisoners of war.

Federal troops acting on the Indian Removal Act forced the Georgia Cherokees—more than 15,000 people—to leave for Oklahoma, a march of more than 800 miles in freezing weather. At least 4,000 Cherokees died on the route, which the Indians called the Trail of Tears. Over the next several years, the United States forced about 70,000 Creeks, Seminoles, Sacs, Foxes, and other groups to leave their homes and go to places without much food, water, or shelter.

Speaking Out for Native Americans

A few white Americans had always objected to the treatment of the Indians. "They would have been safer among the ancient heathens with whom the rites of hospitality were sacred [than among] our frontier people," Benjamin Franklin said in 1764. George Washington felt much the same way: "The frequent destruction of innocent [Native American] women and children," he told Congress in 1795, "continues to shock humanity." Even some men who killed Indians had second thoughts. "Our treatment of the Indians is an outrage," admitted General George Crook, who had led many attacks on Indians, in 1878.

But it took 1881's *A Century of Dishonor* by novelist and poet Helen Hunt Jackson to inspire pro-Indian sentiment. The book exposed government abuse of the Indians, corruption and cruelty of white settlers, bloody massacres, and more. The book attracted enough attention to shift some laws and court cases in the Indians' favor. It marked the beginnings of a shift in American opinion against removing Indians or wiping them out.

In 1849, the government moved the Bureau of Indian Affairs from the War Department to the Interior Department (in charge of land and natural resources), but policies against the Indians remained as warlike as ever. Although at first the government uprooted tribes in the East and moved them west, it now was removing such western tribes as the Minnesota Sioux, Arizona Navajos, and Washington Puyallups.

Whites killed off entire tribes of American Indians like these photographed at their teepee in what is now Glacier National Park, Montana.

At other times, the federal forces simply killed Indians—children, women, and men. Those who survived faced a life of poverty, filth, and disease on reservations.

The members of the House of Representatives were jealous. They weren't jealous of the Indians; they were jealous of the Senate. "[The President] shall have power, with advice and consent of the Senate, to make treaties, provided two-thirds of the Senators present concur," stated the Constitution's Article II. The system left out House members, and they hated it.

To make them happy, Congress killed the whole treaty-making process. "No Indian nation or tribe within the territory of the United States shall be acknowledged or recognized as an independent nation, tribe, or power with whom the United States may contract by treaty," read 1871's Indian Appropriations Act. From then on, the government wouldn't make treaties. It broke all 300-plus previous treaties, as well as laws that respected the Indians. A change was coming, though.

It started on the Rosebud Indian Reservation, in the hilly, high plains of what is now the southern edge of South Dakota, near the Nebraska border. Crow Dog, a Sioux and a former police captain, killed Spotted Tail, a Sioux leader. A Sioux court told Crow Dog to pay Spotted Tail's family enough to support them as Spotted Tail would have.

The area's federal district attorney felt that the sentence wasn't harsh enough. He arrested Crow Dog. A federal court sentenced Crow Dog to death.

Not so fast, said the Supreme Court. In *Ex Parte Crow Dog* (1883), the Court ordered the government to let Crow Dog free. If an Indian killed another Indian on Indian land, Indian courts were in charge.

White America screamed. Outraged that Indian law trumped the laws of the United States, Congress passed the Major Crimes Act of 1885. "All Indians committing against the person or property of another Indian or other person any of the following crimes, namely murder, manslaughter [unintentional murder], rape, assault with the intent to kill, burglary, larceny, and arson, within any territory of the United States . . . shall be subject therefor to the laws of said territory" and not the laws of the tribes.

Two years later, Congress passed the General Allotment Act of 1887, written by Massachusetts senator Henry Dawes. The Dawes Act intended to break up at least some reservations. "In all cases where any tribe or band of Indians has been, or shall hereafter be, located upon any reservation," the Act stated, "the President of the United States [shall] . . . allot the lands in said reservations . . . to any Indian located thereon." Each Indian family would get a plot of 160 acres, or about half a mile on each side—roughly the size of an average American family farm at the time.

The Act also tried to mix Indians into the white majority culture. So the government handed a significant amount of reservation land to whites.

The Dawes Act flopped. Many if not most Indians didn't want to live like whites or be surrounded by them. Sharp and often crooked businessmen swooped in to grab Indian land. The indigenous peoples went from having more than 139 million acres in 1881 to fewer than 53 million in 1900 and fewer than 30 million by 1934.

While Congress moved against the Indians, the Supreme Court ruled for them in the case of *Talton v. Mayes* (1896).

Wash Mayes, a sheriff of the Cherokee Nation, arrested an Indian named Bob Talton for murdering another Cherokee on the reservation. Cherokee laws allowed a five-person jury to hear trials, and a Cherokee jury convicted Talton.

The laws of the United States demanded a larger jury, so Talton sued, claiming that the Cherokees had convicted him illegally. Again, the problem came down to which was more important: Indian law or U.S. law.

The Supreme Court decided for the Cherokees. "The crime of murder committed by one Cherokee Indian upon the person of another within the jurisdiction of the Cherokee Nation is . . . clearly not an offense against the United States but an offense against the local laws of the Cherokee Nation," wrote Justice Edward White.

The Court didn't give total power to the Indians. "The Indian tribes are subject to the dominant authority of Congress," White wrote. "Their powers of local self-government are also operated upon and restrained by the general provisions of the Constitution."

Although the federal government could restrain the Indians, the Indians couldn't restrain the government. They couldn't vote because the government had never declared them U.S. citizens. Even though the Constitution's Fourteenth Amendment (1868) stated clearly, "All persons born or naturalized in the United States . . . are citizens of the United States," the law didn't apply to Native Americans.

In 1924, the Indian Citizenship Act finally made Native Americans citizens. The states could still withhold full citizenship, though. Arizona, for instance, wouldn't let Indians vote until 1948.

In general, conditions for Indians remained "deplorable" —or so stated *The Problem of Indian Administration* (1928), better known as the Meriam Report. The federal government had commissioned the University of Chicago's Lewis Meriam, a non-Indian, to study Indian life. His report stated that schools for native children were "grossly inadequate," disease was rampant, babies died at a shockingly high rate, poverty was common, food and housing were meager and filthy, and Indians in general were desperately unhappy.

The report didn't surprise the Indians, but it shook up quite a few whites. After the liberal government of President Franklin Roosevelt took power in 1933, changes began.

The most important was the Indian Reorganization Act of 1934, "to rehabilitate the Indian's economic life." It outlawed the Dawes allotment system. It set up funds for Indian businesses. It outlined a system of Indian self-government, including new tribal constitutions, which the Bureau of Indian Affairs often wrote.

Most tribes approved the IRA, although some Native Americans came to regard it as just another set of government rules. Still, it wiped away decades of destructive laws. What's more, the amount of land under the tribes' control began to rise for the first time in more than 50 years, inching up from fewer than 29.5 million acres in 1933 to more than 35 million in 1939.

Part of this rise came from Native Americans filing claims with the Bureau of Indian Affairs for land that had been stolen from them. Soon, the BIA had more claims than it could handle. To take them on, the federal government established the Indian Claims Commission (ICC) in 1946.

The ICC didn't return land. It just paid off the tribal governments. The commission eventually considered more than 600 claims and paid out more than $800 million. In exchange for the money, which could amount to as little as a few hundred dollars per Native American, the tribes and their members had to give up their rights to the land forever.

Soon the tribes lost not only land but power. The 1950s saw the federal government pursue "termination"—that is, ending the relationship between the government and the tribes. "It is the policy of Congress, as rapidly as possible, to make the Indians within the territorial limits of the United States subject to the same laws and entitled to the same privileges and responsibilities as are applicable to other citizens of the United States, to end their status as wards of the United States, and to grant them all the rights and prerogatives pertaining to American citizenship," announced the House of Representatives Termination Resolution in 1953. The Termination Resolution was only a statement of intention, sort of a warning shot. The cannonball came two weeks later, with Public Law 280.

The federal government had always kept state governments out of tribal affairs. PL 280 changed all that. An act of Congress, the law gave various states jurisdiction over "criminal offenses and civil causes of action [that is, lawsuits] committed or arising on Indian reservations within such states."

PL 280 didn't let the states tax Native American lands or interfere with Indians' "right, privilege, or immunity . . . with respect to hunting, trapping, or fishing." Otherwise, though, it gave the state governments the same power over the Indians as they had over whites.

Hugh Lee, a non-Indian, ran the Ganado Trading Post, a general store on Arizona's Navajo Reservation. Lee said that two of his customers, a Navajo couple named Paul and Lorena Williams, hadn't paid one of their bills. Lee sued them in state court. The Williamses said he couldn't do that, because only the tribal court could rule on transactions and people in the reservations.

In *Williams v. Lee* (1959), the U.S. Supreme Court sided with the Williamses. Letting the state take charge "would undermine the authority of the tribal courts over reservation affairs and hence would infringe on the right of the Indians to govern themselves," wrote Justice Hugo Black. Tribal law had beaten state law.

Although the Supreme Court gave the tribes more power, Congress took some of it away. The American Indian Civil Rights Act of 1968 limited the power of tribal courts and leaders in the same way that the Bill of Rights limited the federal government. It directed the tribes not to block Native American freedom of speech or press, deny any Indian a fair trial by jury, try him twice for the same crime, force him to be a witness against himself, take his property without paying for it, search his home or body, inflict cruel and unusual punishment on him, or discriminate against him.

Five years later, the Supreme Court stood up again for Native American rights. Rosalind McClanahan had an Irish name, but she was a Navajo living and working on an Arizona Navajo reservation. Arizona collected some taxes by taking them out of worker paychecks. In 1967, the state took $16.20 from McClanahan's checks. She sued, saying the

The American Indian Movement

In 1968, a group of Native Americans in Minneapolis formed the American Indian Movement (AIM), to speak out for Native American rights. In 1969, AIM members took over Alcatraz, the former prison on an island near San Francisco, claiming that by treaty, unused federal land belonged to Native Americans. In 1972, AIM took over the Bureau of Indian Affairs Building in Washington, DC. The next year, the group grabbed Wounded Knee, South Dakota, the site of an Indian massacre in 1890. AIM is no longer the force that it was, but it has helped enlighten people about Native Americans.

state had no right to tax a Navajo who earned her living on a Navajo reservation.

"[McClanahan's] rights as a reservation Indian were violated when the state collected a tax from her which it had no jurisdiction to impose," said Justice Thurgood Marshall in *McClanahan v. Arizona State Tax Commission* (1973). "By imposing the tax . . . the state has interfered with matters which the relevant treaty and statutes leave to the exclusive province of the federal government and the Indians themselves."

In 1975, Congress stepped in again. For decades, the Bureau of Indian Affairs should have ensured Native education, health, law enforcement and other benefits.

It didn't. "The prolonged federal domination of Indian service programs has served to retard rather than enhance the progress of Indian people and their communities by depriving Indians of the full opportunity to develop leadership skills crucial to the realization of self-government," stated the Indian Self-Determination and Education Assistance Act of 1975. To help Native Americans rule themselves rather than depend on the federal government, the Act, passed on January 4, gave the tribes more power over a considerable range of services, plus some money to help them pay for the services.

Seventeen days later, the Supreme Court increased the power of tribal government even further in *United States v. Mazurie*. White saloonkeepers Martin and Margaret Mazurie had opened the Blue Bull bar on Wyoming's Wind River reservation. One problem: The reservation's Tribal council refused to give them a license to open the bar. The Mazuries claimed that the council had no legal right to stop them.

They were wrong. Native American tribes, Justice William Rehnquist wrote, "possess a certain degree of independent authority over matters that affect the internal and social relations of tribal life."

Despite the Court's rulings, the state governments didn't quit trying to rule the tribes.

In the 1970s, tribes and other Native American groups started to open and run casinos. Some states hated having unregulated gambling in their midst. Religious conservatives considered gambling immoral; other citizens worried that casinos would attract gangsters and other ugly elements.

So in 1988, Congress passed the Indian Gaming Regulatory Act. Under the law, a tribe had to negotiate with its state government to decide the kinds of gambling that the casinos would offer. The law also set up the National Indian Gaming Commission to make everyone involved obey the law.

Only a tiny minority of tribes had casinos. Crime, illness, unemployment, poverty, and other problems were still generally much higher among Native Americans than among whites. The Bureau of Indian Affairs owed the tribes millions of dollars from companies using the oil, minerals, and forests on Indian lands. And in 1988, President Ronald Reagan showed a remarkable ignorance of Native American attitudes and history when he said, "Maybe we made a mistake in trying to maintain Indian cultures. Maybe we should not have humored them in wanting to stay in that kind of primitive lifestyle."

Even the Supreme Court turned against the tribes. In *Brendale v. Confederated Tribes & Bands of the Yakima Indian Nations* (1989), the Court said tribes couldn't control areas of their reservations that they had neglected and that non-Indians had bought. *Duro v. Reina* (1990) said a tribe couldn't arrest, convict, or imprison non-members who committed crimes on the tribe's reservation. In 1990's *Employment Division of Oregon v. Smith*, the Court said that Native Americans couldn't use illegal narcotics in religious ceremonies that had traditionally used the drugs. *Seminole Tribe of Florida v. [State of] Florida* (1996) decreed that a tribe couldn't sue a state government for blocking the tribe from establishing a casino.

Congress passed laws to overturn or weaken the *Duro* and *Oregon* decisions. In October 1990, it approved the Native American Languages Act to "preserve, protect, and promote the rights and freedom of Native Americans to use, practice, and develop Native American languages." A few weeks later, Congress passed the Native American Graves Protection and Repatriation Act. It protected Native grave sites and forced museums holding ancient Indian property, including dead bodies, to give them back to the tribes.

As Congress and the Court have made their decisions, Native Americans have continued to battle poverty and racism. There has even been an ongoing fight to change the names of sports teams such as the Washington Redskins.

Some things have at least seemed to get better. In late 2000, the Bureau of Indian Affairs made overtures to Native Americans. "Never again will we attack your religions, your languages, your rituals, or any of your tribal ways," said Kevin Gover, the BIA's head and a Pawnee Indian.

The words sounded good. Not even Gover knew for sure, however, whether the United States ever would hand over full rights and justice to the people who had lived on the land first.

4 Immigrants

When Christopher Columbus landed in the Caribbean islands in 1492, he launched an age of immigration. In 1565, Pedro Menendez de Aviles—described as both a Spanish admiral and a smuggler leading a ragtag army—established North America's first settlement, the city of St. Augustine.

The English soon caught up. In what was probably America's first clear-cut list of immigrant rights, the colony charter of the Englishmen who landed in Virginia during 1607 gave the settlers the "liberties, franchises, and immunities" that they would have had "in our realm of England."

By the early 1610s, they were inviting other Englishmen to join them. It was possibly the first time that anyone in America actively encouraged immigration.

In 1620, the Pilgrims came over. The members of this Christian church wanted a place where they could practice their religion and outlaw any other. They set up the Massachusetts Bay Colony.

Still, even the stodgy Pilgrims seemed to accept outsiders. "Every person within this jurisdiction, whether inhabitant or foreigner, shall enjoy the same justice and law," stated the Massachusetts Body of Liberties (1641).

Although some immigrants came to America for religious reasons, some were convicts that European countries simply dumped in the New World. Others came to find jobs or cheap land. Quite a few made the trip as indentured servants, hired by employers who would pay for their journey if the newcomers would work under them for years until the price of the trip was paid off.

However they came, there were many. From the settlement of St. Augustine in 1565, to the signing of the Declaration of Independence in 1776, about one million immigrants came to America. During the short stretch of time from the end of the French and Indian War in 1763, to the start of the Revolutionary War in 1775, another million immigrants arrived, bringing the colonies' population to 2.2 million.

The new nation quickly set rules for its newcomers. Written in 1787, the Constitution's Article II stated, "The Congress shall have power . . . to establish a uniform rule of naturalization." (Naturalization is the process of letting immigrants become citizens.) The Naturalization Act of 1790 added, "[Only] a free white person who shall have resided within the limits and under the jurisdiction of the United States for the term of two years may be admitted to become a citizen." Because nonwhite immigrants such as Asians and Africans couldn't become citizens, they couldn't vote or exercise other powers of citizenship.

Even immigrants who could become citizens faced hard times. In 1795, a new Naturalization Act decreed that to become a citizen, an immigrant had to live in the United States for five years, far longer than the two years of the 1790 act.

What was the reason for the change? For one thing, Americans were getting scared. Violent revolutionaries were shaking up Ireland, Italy, Poland, Haiti, and other countries. North African nations were raiding American vessels. France, which was overrunning most of Europe under the leadership of Napoleon Bonaparte, ordered its own sea-going fleet to grab American ships. Many Americans considered foreigners dangerous.

In 1798, America was so panicky that Congress passed one antiforeign law after another. The Naturalization Act of 1798 stated that five years of living in the United States wasn't enough to make a foreigner a citizen and raised the rule to fourteen years. The Alien Act let the president take any foreigner whom he considered a danger to the United States and banish him from the country. The Alien Enemies Act allowed the government to kick out any aliens—even those who became citizens—if they had come from a country hostile to the United States. Thomas Jefferson, who ran for president in 1800, called the acts "worthy of the eighth or ninth century."

After Jefferson became president, the government let the Alien Act expire. The Naturalization Act of 1802 repealed the 1798 measure and returned the residency requirement to five years. The Alien Enemies Act stayed on the books, but the government usually ignored it. After 1815, the wars in Europe subsided.

Newcomers flooded in like water from a fire hose. Immigration rose from around 10,000 in 1820 to nearly 40 times that amount in 1850. "As many people arrived in the 1840s (17 million) as had come in the 230 preceding years," writes journalist Tod Olson.

The biggest wave of immigrants came from Ireland. For years, the desperately poor Irish had survived by farming potatoes. In 1845, a disease killed the crop. Hundreds of thousands of Irish people came to America, settling largely in the northeast from Massachusetts through Pennsylvania.

No Irish Need Apply. That sign faced immigrants looking for work. Native-born Americans were scared that the Irish immigrants would take their jobs. What's more, the Irish were Catholic, and most Americans were Protestant. Philadelphians rioted against the Irish. Mobs in Boston burned Catholic convents.

While the Irish had trouble in the East, Chinese immigrants hit problems out west. In 1848, after gold was discovered in California, the state attracted hordes of newcomers. Thousands of them were poor Chinese.

California's white population didn't want the Chinese. In 1850, the state government blocked nonwhites from voting and imposed taxes, fees, and restrictions on foreign miners, especially Chinese miners. They kept coming anyway, as did the Irish, Germans, Scandinavians, and British.

If California imposed special taxes on Chinese immigrants, or other states allowed discrimination against the Irish, that was their own business. The federal government didn't get involved until 1849's *Smith v. Turner* and *Norris v. Boston*, known as the Passenger Cases.

Fighting Racial Hatred

As Irish Catholics flooded into America after 1845, a new, anti-immigrant, anti-Catholic political party arose. It had several names: the American Republican Party (no relation to the modern Republican Party), the Native American Party (no relation to the indigenous peoples), and the Know-Nothings (for their refusal to discuss their policies).

The party became so prominent that Abraham Lincoln was moved to attack it in 1855: "As a nation, we began by declaring that all men are created equal . . . When the Know-Nothings get control, it will read, 'All men are created equal, except Negroes and foreigners and Catholics.' When it comes to this, I should prefer emigrating to some country where they make no pretense of loving liberty—to Russia, for instance, where despotism can be taken pure, and without the base alloy of hypocrisy."

To discourage ships from bringing in immigrants, some states taxed the ships for each passenger. Although the Supreme Court struck down the tax, saying the states couldn't discourage all immigration, it did let the states reject "paupers, vagabonds, and fugitives from justice," as Justice James Wayne wrote. "The states may meet such persons upon their arrival in port, and may put them under all proper restraints. They may prevent them from entering their territories, may carry them out or drive them off."

61

Still the immigrants poured in. The 1840s had averaged about 170,000 a year, and the rate hit 300,000 in the late 1860s.

Once an immigrant got in, a state could stop him from owning "real property"—land or buildings—if the state did the same to all other immigrants. "State legislation applying alike and equally to all aliens, withholding from them the right to own land, cannot be said to be capricious or to amount to an arbitrary deprivation of liberty or property," said Supreme Court Justice Stephen Field in *Phillips v. Moore* (1879).

Despite such restrictions, immigrants kept coming, and more than ever: more than 600,000 in 1881 and nearly 800,000 the next year. It was the start of a trend called the Great Migration (or sometimes, the First Great Migration), which would bring more than 25 million Russians, Poles, Italians, Greeks, and others to American shores by 1924.

Congress tried to stop them. The Immigration Act of 1882 put a federal tax on every immigrant. It also outlawed the immigration of convicts, the insane, paupers, and other people who were likely to be a danger or a drain on society.

That same year, Congress passed an even tougher law, the Chinese Exclusion Act. It banned immigration from China, threatened a year in jail and a $500 fine on any skipper or shipmaster who brought Chinese immigrants to America, and decreed that "no state court, or court of the United States, shall admit Chinese to citizenship." Other immigrants kept coming. More than 500,000 arrived in 1891, when anti-immigrant fever blew up into a new Immigration Act. "The following classes of aliens shall be excluded from admission into the United States: all idiots, insane persons, paupers, or persons likely to become a public charge"—that is, people who couldn't take care of themselves and had to depend on government aid. The act also stopped criminals, any man with more than one wife, and people with "loathsome or contagious disease." It blocked employers from advertising overseas for foreign workers or paying their way to America. It ordered the government to deport anyone who entered the country illegally. It let the federal government inspect and patrol the United States' borders with Mexico and Canada. It set up the first federal immigration department, known today as the Immigration and Naturalization Service, to examine and inspect all immigrants.

Immigrants kept arriving, and in growing numbers. The year 1905 was the first time that more than one million people entered the country in a single year. In 1907 came the biggest wave of immigration that the United States had ever seen and the biggest that it would see until 1990: nearly 1.3 million, mostly from Eastern Europe and Italy.

In all, the new century's first decade pulled in nearly nine million people, more than any decade before or since. By 1910, nearly 14 million foreign-born people lived in America, making up almost 15 percent of the population—the highest proportion in history. (Today's figure is around 10 percent.)

Move back for a moment to 1859, when biologist Charles Darwin proposed the theory of natural selection. Also called survival of the fittest, the theory stated that some living things are born with traits that help them to survive better than others. Farmers had known about that sort of thing for a while and intentionally mated (for instance) strong horses with each other to breed an entire line of strong horses.

In 1893, English scientist Francis Galton applied Darwin's ideas to people and created a system that he called eugenics. Humans, he thought, could choose each other for certain traits and breed to preserve and strengthen those traits. They might also discourage individuals with negative traits—for instance, low intelligence or inherited diseases—from reproducing. The idea went back to ancient Greece, but now it sounded like science.

Eugenics traveled to the United States. In 1894, the idea inspired a group called the Immigration Restriction League. The IRL and other groups claimed that immigrants were inferior breeding stock and should not get into the country.

By America's entry into World War I in 1917, the ideas had infected top politicians, college professors, and heads of major corporations. Respected scientists freely called the recent waves of Italians, Russians, and Poles "moral cripples" or "hirsute, low-browed . . . ox-like men," inferior to the English and Dutch who were among America's earliest settlers. They often considered Asians even worse.

Eugenics wasn't the only trend against immigrants. Communism was a fairly new political philosophy that attacked American institutions such as business and religion. A Communist revolution swept over Russia in 1917. Also that year, the United States entered World War I on the side of England and against Germany. Suddenly, anyone from central Europe (home of Germany) or Eastern Europe (Russia's region) seemed not just alien but evil.

"Our capacity to maintain our cherished institutions stands diluted by a stream of alien blood," said Congressman Albert Johnson, a chief author of the Immigration Act of

1924. The act allowed in only 2 percent of each nationality that was in the country in 1890. If there were 100,000 French-born people in the United States during 1890, then only 2,000 French people could enter each year. (After 1929, the quota would be based on the 1920 census.)

The law completely barred anyone who couldn't become a citizen, such as Asians. It imposed no limit on immigrants from the Americas, although it set up the Border Patrol to stop undocumented foreigners (today called illegal aliens). It set up an entry-visa system; anyone who wanted to immigrate had to get written permission (a visa) from an American diplomat in the immigrant's country. It ordered that starting in 1929, the annual number of immigrants must drop to 150,000—little more than a tenth of the 1907 figure.

The First Great Migration was over. That wasn't the end of bad news for the foreign-born, though.

On December 7, 1941, Japanese planes bombed Hawaii's Pearl Harbor and the attack propelled the United States into World War II (1939–1945). On February 19, 1942, President Franklin Roosevelt signed Executive Order 9066, which told Secretary of War Henry Stimson to designate "military areas . . . from which any or all persons may be excluded."

General John DeWitt, in charge of the defense of the West Coast, hated the Japanese—even Japanese Americans. "They are a dangerous element," he said. "A Jap's a Jap . . . It makes no difference if he is an American; theoretically, he is still Japanese, and you can't change him." DeWitt used Roosevelt's decree to pull almost 120,000 Japanese Americans from their homes. He imprisoned them in internment camps, even though Attorney General Francis Biddle confessed that among the thousands of prisoners, "We have not uncovered . . . any dangerous persons."

While DeWitt imprisoned the Japanese, America's farmers needed bodies. Young farmhands were leaving the hot, dusty fields for military service or for high-paying jobs in factories making military supplies. Meanwhile, unemployed farm workers in Mexico needed work.

In August 1942, the United States and Mexico joined to start the Bracero program (from the Spanish word *brazo*, or arm). The Braceros were Mexican farmworkers who would work American farms and then return to Mexico. "Mexicans entering the United States as result of this understanding shall not suffer discriminatory acts of any kind," stated the agreement between the governments. "Wages to be paid the workers shall be the same as those paid for similar work to other agricultural laborers . . . The Mexican workers will be furnished without cost to them with hygienic lodgings . . . [and] medical and sanitary services." The number of Mexican workers in the United States leaped from about 4,200 in 1942 to more than 50,000 the next year.

Unfortunately, the Braceros didn't get what the agreement offered. They often faced low wages, racist harassment, and filthy lodgings and working conditions.

The immigration scene wasn't all gloom. Because China was fighting Japan and was therefore an American ally, Congress repealed the laws against Chinese immigration in December 1943. For the first time in more than sixty years, the Chinese could enter the United States; for the first time ever, they could become full citizens. Still, Congress allowed in only a tiny number of Chinese: 105 people per year.

Exactly a year later, President Roosevelt lifted the imprisonment of Japanese Americans. However, they couldn't simply return to their old lives. During their internment, they hadn't been able to protect their homes and businesses, and many were lost to them.

After World War II ended in 1945, anti-immigrant bias started to slip away. In military service and at home, native-born Americans had served alongside immigrants and the children of immigrants and could see that they were good people. Besides, the government had been urging all Americans to pull together to defeat the enemy forces. One of the enemies was the Germans, who had called themselves the "master race" and taken eugenics to the extreme by working to wipe out other nationalities. As a result, it was hard for Americans to despise immigrants as openly as they had in the first part of the century.

All was not so rosy for long. In 1949, the Russians—still under communism—blew up an atomic bomb. Atomic bombs are so powerful that America had defeated Japan in World War II using only two of them.

Many Americans considered the Russians too backward for such an advanced feat. Someone in America must have given them the bomb's secrets. Foreigners were prime suspects.

In 1950, Congress passed the Internal Security Act, spearheaded by Nevada senator Patrick McCarran. Among other things, the act ordered the government to block the entry of immigrants who had ever had a connection to Communism or other "un-American" movements, and to deport those who had already entered.

McCarran struck again in 1952. The Immigration and Nationality Act banned East Asian immigrants. It preserved the quota system of the 1920s and in some ways deepened it: The new law gave greater preference to skilled workers and northern Europeans.

President Harry Truman called the act "utterly unworthy of our traditions and ideals." It became law anyway. In retaliation, Truman created a commission on immigration that would have a huge effect in the mid-1960s.

By that time, immigration was changing again. Take the Bracero program. In 1961, nearly 300,000 migrants had been involved; the next year, the figure dropped to less than 200,000, and kept falling. In 1964, the program ended—it took with it a way for hundreds of thousands of Mexicans to enter the United States legally.

But the biggest change came the next year. Truman's immigration commission had recommended changes that formed the skeleton of the Immigration Act of 1965. The act eliminated most quotas and permitted 290,000 immigrants per year.

The government soon enacted exceptions to the law, which allowed in even more immigrants. The Cuban Refugee Act of 1966 made it easier for refugees from communist Cuba to become citizens. Another measure in 1980 opened the door to more than 100,000 additional fleeing Cubans. After the Vietnam War ended in the 1970s, the government let in large numbers of Cambodians and Vietnamese. The Refugee Act of 1980 said up to 50,000 people every year could enter the United States for "grave humanitarian reasons."

Still, the government blocked plenty of others from entering legally, so they entered illegally; especially Latin Americans. By the end of the 1970s, at least 2.5 million illegal aliens were living in the United States.

America's labor unions worried that the flood of immigrants would compete with union members for jobs. They pushed Congress to pass the Immigration Reform and Control Act of 1986.

The law meant to slam the door on new illegal aliens while showing mercy to those already in the country. It outlawed hiring illegal aliens, slapping a fine of up to $10,000 on any employer who hired them. On the other hand, the law offered amnesty—that is, freedom from arrest—for illegal aliens already in the United States. The law also created up to 15,000 entry visas for new immigrants.

Immigration shot straight up. By 1990, almost 20 million foreign-born people lived in America, and more were coming. More than 1.5 million immigrants entered the country in 1990 and more than 1.8 million in 1991—the biggest yearly totals in American history. (Even with those numbers, immigrants accounted for only about 8 percent of the population—approximately half the percentage of 1910.)

The numbers would stay high with the Immigration Act of 1990. The new law upped the number of legal immigrants allowed into the United States from the 1965 Immigration Act's 290,000 per year to 825,000.

The act gave special preference to skilled workers, especially "aliens with extraordinary ability, outstanding professors and researchers, [and] multinational executives and managers." The government granted these workers—65,000 per year—a work permit called an H-1B visa. It would become a powerful tool in making some Americans very rich.

But immigration, especially illegal immigration, still troubled plenty of Americans. In 1996, President Bill Clinton signed bills that changed immigrant life yet again.

The Personal Responsibility and Work Opportunity Reconciliation Act took welfare benefits from millions of immigrants, both legal and illegal.

The Antiterrorism and Effective Death Penalty Act empowered the government to kick out any aliens that it suspected of terrorism. The aliens couldn't fight those deportations, because the government could keep the evidence against them secret, even from the immigrants themselves.

The Illegal Immigration Reform and Immigrant Responsibility Act allowed the immigration service to deport any immigrant who had committed a state or federal crime, even if the immigrant had already served his sentence. The law also blocked the immigrant from getting a trial or hearing to fight the deportation. If an immigrant's home country wouldn't take him back, the United States would put him in prison until the situation changed—which might never happen.

After these acts went into effect, immigration dropped from more than 900,000 in 1996 to almost 800,000 the next year to under 700,000 in 1998 (the most recent year that the government has covered).

At the same time, though, high-tech businesses have been hungry for computer programmers, engineers, and other scientifically skilled workers. They have used as many H-1B visas as they can, and have pressured Congress to raise the annual rate of H-1B visas from 65,000 to 115,000 per year.

Immigrants, who had survived treacherous journeys to come to America, arrived only to face the hatred and cruelty of discrimination.

However, the Immigration and Naturalization Service has been backlogged with applications for entry visas and naturalization. Processing an application can take years.

What's more, the service has only 8,000 border agents to patrol the 2,000-mile border between the United States and Mexico. Consequently, hundreds of thousands of people slip illegally into the United States every year.

To fix the situation, a proposal began floating around Congress to break up the INS into two agencies, one to handle visa applications and other important paperwork, and one to enforce the immigration laws with border patrols and other methods.

Despite the barriers in front of them, immigrants keep coming. Most are not well educated. They need welfare and other assistance programs more often than native-born Americans do. They're less healthy and less able to make their way in American society than the native-born. Because most of them are not white and don't speak English, they face racism and job discrimination. No matter what, though, they still want to come to America.

5 Prisoners

A man grabs you from behind, jabs a gun in the back of your neck, shoves his hand in your pockets, and steals your money. What rights and freedoms does he deserve?

You might say he doesn't deserve the freedom to amble around as he likes. You'd put him in prison.

Should the prison give him freedom of speech? Should he have the right to vote? Should he be free from torture and other painful punishments?

Should he even have the right to keep breathing? Imprisoning him may kill him in prison-yard fights, filthy and diseased living conditions, or with a lethal injection.

Prisoners' rights always have been a complicated and messy area. In past centuries, quite a few judges, kings, and laws demanded killing or mutilation for even small crimes. Others ejected the guilty from their place in the community (a punishment called civil death), banished them, or threw them into slavery or prison. They also got thrown into debt:

Criminals could pay for some crimes—especially theft or destruction of property—by paying the same amount in money or property to the victim.

Whether the criminal suffered prison, pain, or payment, the law always meant the punishments to fit the crime. In 1215, England's Magna Carta stated plainly, "A freeman shall not be amerced [that is, fined or punished] for a slight offense, except in accordance with the degree of the offense; and for a grave offense he shall be amerced in accordance with the gravity of the offense."

Later regimes strengthened these rights. The English Bill of Rights (1689) stated, among other things, "Excessive bail [a fee to spring from jail the people who were accused but not yet convicted] ought not to be required, nor excessive fines imposed; nor cruel and unusual punishment inflicted." Some of this language would show up again more than a century later.

English settlers carried their country's traditions to the New World. The Massachusetts Body of Liberties (1641) stated, "For bodily punishments, we allow amongst us none that are inhumane, barbarous, or cruel."

Death was one punishment that they didn't consider inhuman, barbarous, or cruel. "If any man . . . shall have or worship any other god but the Lord God, he shall be put to death," stated the Body of Liberties. "If any man rise up by false witness, wittingly and of purpose, to take away another man's life, he shall be put to death."

For punishments short of death, local authorities didn't put the guilty in prison. America didn't have many prisons, though it did have jails to hold people who were

The Eighth Amendment

Before it became law, the Bill of Rights triggered arguments. But one right that most agreed on was the Eighth Amendment's rule against cruel and unusual punishment. One of the few objections came from Congressman Samuel Livermore of New Hampshire. "It is sometimes necessary to hang a man; villains often deserve whipping and perhaps having their ears cut off; but are we, in [the] future, to be prevented from inflicting these punishments because they are cruel? If a more lenient mode of correcting vice and deterring others from the commission of it could be invented, it would be very prudent in the legislature to adopt it, but until we have some security that this will be done, we ought not to be restrained from making necessary laws [and punishments]."

arrested and awaiting trial. Instead, the authorities whipped prisoners or branded them with a spitting-hot iron. There were also the stocks, wooden frames that trapped prisoners by the hands, feet, and head in a bent-over position for days at a time.

By the end of the 1700s, some people may have thought that these punishments were a tad harsh. In 1791, for instance, the Constitution's Eighth Amendment read, "Excessive bail shall not be required, nor excessive fines imposed, nor cruel and unusual punishments inflicted." It echoed the English Bill of Rights almost word for word.

England contributed another idea, too. English political reformer Jeremy Bentham proposed that prison should be "a mill for grinding rogues honest and idle men industrious"— that is, it should not just confine criminals but also reform them into productive citizens.

Some of Bentham's methods are still around. In his day, prison authorities simply dumped groups of prisoners into a single room. If a prisoner had privacy, he could think about his crimes and change his ways—or so Bentham thought. So he more or less invented the modern prison cell and solitary confinement.

Yet another trend grew up in Philadelphia. The town had plenty of Quakers, a group of Protestants who promoted equality and nonviolence. Like Bentham, the Quakers believed in lonely meditation to make a criminal turn good, and productive work to make him a solid citizen.

The Quakers convinced the local government to turn those ideas—especially solitary confinement—into reality in a jail on Philadelphia's Walnut Street. Each prisoner had his own cell where he lived and worked alone, day and night.

Other states and cities began to copy the Walnut Street approach. The nation turned away from killing and torturing prisoners, and turned toward putting them in penitentiaries (places for people to be penitent or sorry for what they'd done).

With one cell per prisoner, the prisons soon had more inmates than cells. Walnut Street became overcrowded.

By 1820, a new approach showed up in the town of Auburn, New York. Auburn was (and is) a small city southwest of Syracuse. Its prison's cells—seven feet long, three and one-half feet wide, and seven feet high, about the size of a walk-in closet—were smaller than the Walnut Street cells, so it could cram more cells and prisoners into a similar area.

Auburn could use small cells because the prisoners didn't have to live in them at every moment. Each man was alone in his cell at night but during the daytime working hours the prisoners labored in groups.

They labored hard. The prisoners' keeper (the title of warden wasn't commonly used yet), Elam Lynds, a former Revolutionary War army captain, tightly scheduled every moment of their lives. He wouldn't let prisoners talk, even at work or meals. To get from place to place, prisoners had to march in "lockstep," forming a slow and tightly packed chain of men with their heads and arms turned so that they couldn't talk or gesture to each other.

Then as now, "inmates were not entitled to life, liberty, and the pursuit of happiness," wrote prison expert Scott Christianson in his book *With Liberty for Some: 500 Years of Imprisonment in America.* "A prisoner did not enjoy the free exercise of religion or freedom of speech or of the press, or the right to assemble peaceably . . . Inmates could be penalized without due process of law . . . [and] their private property was taken from them."

If a prisoner didn't like this treatment, too bad. Lynds gave his assistants tentacled whips to use on any prisoner who stepped even slightly out of line. He locked the worst offenders in solitary confinement.

Auburn's system became more influential than the Walnut Street way. The problems of prisoners faded from public attention. For decades, few major national laws dealt with prisoners. Those that did, such as the Constitution's Thirteenth Amendment (1865)—"Neither slavery nor involuntary servitude, except as a punishment for crime whereof the party shall have been duly convicted, shall exist within the United States"—reinforced the idea of convicts as virtual slaves with no rights at all.

An exception came in the Civil Rights Act of 1871. "Any person who, under cover of any law . . . shall subject, or cause to be subjected, any person . . . to the deprivation of any rights, privileges, or immunities secured by the Constitution of the United States, shall . . . be liable to the party [he has deprived]." If a cop or prison guard violated another person's civil rights, the victim could sue; that is, unless he couldn't. "Convicts generally were not allowed to write (or in later years, to mail) letters to outsiders, including the courts, unless they had been specifically approved by the prison warden," wrote Christianson. "Even if convicts somehow had managed to get through to the courts with their complaints, judges and their clerks typically turned a deaf ear."

By the mid-1870s, though, it was clear that the Auburn and Walnut Street systems didn't do what they were supposed to do—reform criminals. It was especially clear to Zebulon Brockway.

Brockway was a radical, young warden from Detroit. He wanted to let prison officials decide when to release criminals depending on their behavior behind bars, a plan called the indeterminate sentence. The state legislature blocked him, so he quit.

He moved to New York State, where legislators were more open to prison reform. In 1876, Brockway took over the new state prison at Elmira, a town just north of the Pennsylvania border.

Elmira Reformatory ushered in a new era of prison reform to help rehabilitate and educate prisoners instead of merely punishing them.

Elmira Reformatory was not for hard-bitten, old, career criminals but for first-time offenders aged sixteen to thirty. Brockway wanted to steer them away from crime before it was too late. He used military discipline as much as Elam Lynds had, but he also offered education, indeterminate sentences, and parole, the new practice of letting prisoners out early if they stayed in touch with prison officials and kept out of trouble.

Brockway's ideas spread to other prisons, but they weren't the era's only trend. Prisons still kept prisoners hard at work, so it was only natural that prison officials would use the work to pay for their food and housing.

Convict labor had been around for a long time. It may even have built the Pyramids and other government buildings. In the last half of the nineteenth century, prisons signed contracts with private businesses to supply them with labor at a cheap price. By 1885, contract labor involved more than 100 prisons and 50,000 prisoners.

The contract labor system wasn't easy anywhere, but it was especially harsh in southern states. Hard labor in prisons in those states worked convicts literally to death at three times the rate of those in the north. During the early 1880s, Louisiana novelist George Washington Cable wrote articles publicly attacking the setup as "a disgrace to civilization." "It kills like a pestilence, teaches the people to be cruel, sets up a false system of clemency, and seduces the state into the committal of murder for money," he said. His reports shocked millions of people.

The rising union labor movement didn't like the contract system, either. Prisons charged lower wages than union laborers did, so businessmen either hired prisoners and fired unionists or didn't hire unionists at all. Under pressure from unions, humanitarians, and others, the use of prison labor in business started to shrink in the late 1880s.

The South soon threw in another twist. The Civil War (1861–1865) had destroyed black slavery in the southern states, and the Fifteenth Amendment (1870) gave black men the right to vote. White southerners were furious.

Most states didn't (and most still don't) allow prisoners or former prisoners to vote, depending on the crimes that they committed. Removing the vote from people is called disenfranchisement. Southern states aimed it at blacks.

"Mississippi led the way in 1890 by replacing a constitutional provision disenfranchising citizens convicted of 'any crime' with a narrower section barring only those

6 Gays and Lesbians

It started with the Bible. "Thou shalt not lie with mankind as with womankind" is written in Leviticus, chapter 18. It was repeated two chapters later. "If a man lie with mankind as with womankind, both of them have committed abomination: they shall surely be put to death."

The Bible didn't say much if anything about women lying with womankind—that is, lesbians—but the message was clear: Gay relationships are wrong and deserve punishment.

Not everyone felt that way. Ancient Greek societies sometimes accepted love between men. For soldiers, some philosophers felt, gay love was a good thing, because it bonded the men together.

Christianity looked down on homosexuality. Although Jesus didn't say anything about it, his disciple Paul called gay love shameful and insisted that gay men deserve punishment in Romans, chapter 1. In First Corinthians, chapter 6, he added, "Neither the immoral, nor idolators, nor homosexuals . . . will inherit the Kindgom of God."

As Christianity began to spread over Europe during the first centuries AD, Paul's attitudes went with it. Christian kings flatly outlawed homosexuality and often ordered death for gays.

Things stayed that way for more than a thousand years. In 1566, Spanish authorities in Florida executed a Frenchman for committing homosexual acts—possibly the first conviction for homosexuality in what would become the United States. In 1610, the English colony of Virginia passed America's first known law against homosexuality. Again, the punishment was death.

Twenty-six years later, the Massachusetts Bay Colony passed its own law decreeing death for gays. It was probably the country's first law to forbid gay acts among women as well as men. Other colonies and communities passed similar laws.

When the United States became an independent nation in 1776, antigay feeling didn't change, although the death penalty was becoming less standard. In 1778, the Continental army kicked out but didn't kill a Lieutenant Enslin for "attempting to commit sodomy." (Sodomy is another name for homosexual acts.)

The English-speaking world generally considered gay love a crime against the laws of man, God, and nature. It was so forbidden that most people never discussed it. Gay relationships were called "the love that dare not speak its name."

In 1897, a small crack began to show in the thick wall of silence. *Sexual Inversion* by English psychologist Havelock Ellis stunned people who read it. Unlike almost everyone else in the past several centuries, Ellis didn't treat

English psychologist Havelock Ellis was one of the first scholars to realize that people are born gay.

homosexuality as a crime, a sin, or a disease, but simply as a fact. He declared that some people were born gay, just as others were born straight, and that nearly everyone has both homosexual and heterosexual feelings.

Slowly and carefully, some gay men and lesbians began to form a community or two. New York's Greenwich Village neighborhood, for instance, embraced all kinds of people (and still does). Starting around 1910, it featured gay nightclubs, bars, and other hangouts.

In the mid-1920s, World War I veteran Henry Gerber of Illinois, founded the Society for Human Rights, which may have been America's first gay organization. The group didn't last long, but it did put out a magazine—possibly the first to demand freedom for gays.

Still, most of America remained as antigay as ever. The average gay man or lesbian often felt isolated, alone, and afraid to look for another gay person.

After decades of such fear and loneliness, a new race began for gay rights. The starting pistol was fired by a bug doctor.

In the 1920s and 1930s, Indiana zoologist Alfred Kinsey became an expert on the gall wasp, but in the 1940s he turned to studying sex. Starting in 1942, he and his assistants asked more than 5,000 men about their sex lives.

Kinsey's *Sexual Behavior in the Human Male*, published in 1948, caused a sensation. It announced that more than a third of all men—37 percent—had had at least one homosexual experience. About 10 percent were completely gay. To millions of gays who didn't dare mention their desires, the book sent a loud message: You are not alone.

If you know that there are other people like you, then you may try to meet them. That's what Los Angeles actor Harry Hay and other gay Angelenos did in 1950. Taking the name of the secret, all-male groups of European actors who performed behind masks more than 500 years earlier, they founded the Mattachine Society—the first known American gay organization since the Society for Human Rights.

It soon waded neck-deep into trouble. Gay love was still illegal. To catch gays, many an undercover policeman pretended to be gay and looking for a partner. If an unsuspecting gay man offered to lie with him as with womankind, the cop arrested him. Most gay men tried to keep the incident secret.

An Anti-Gay Government

The early 1950s were an ugly time for gay rights. Senator Joseph McCarthy of Wisconsin, chairman of the Senate's Permanent Subcommittee on Investigations, gained enormous power by (among other things) accusing government employees of being gay.

"Homosexuals . . . are not proper persons to be employed in government," read a 1950 Subcommittee report. "Aside from the criminality and immorality involved in sex perversion, such behavior is so contrary to the normal, accepted standards of social behavior that persons who engage in such activity are looked upon as outcasts by society . . . Since the initiation of this investigation, considerable progress has been made in removing homosexuals and similar undesirable employees from . . . positions in government."

Mattachine member Dale Jennings was different. In 1952, the cops arrested him for indecent behavior. He publicly admitted being gay but said he was innocent of any criminal charge.

With the help of other Mattachines, Jennings won his case. It was possibly the first time that an openly gay American had beaten the system.

Two years later, the Mattachines got into another fight. The group published the magazine *One*, which is thought to have been the first gay magazine to be distributed nationwide. In 1954, though, California's U.S. Post Office department dubbed it "obscene, lewd, lascivious, and filthy," and refused to deliver it.

The Mattachines sued and won. In 1958, the Supreme Court ruled that the right to distribute a gay magazine was the law of the land.

Though Jennings and *One* involved gay men, lesbians were starting to get their own spotlight. In 1953, Alfred Kinsey published *Sexual Behavior in the Human Female*. A solid 13 percent of all women had had at least one homosexual experience, the book stated, and at least 2 percent of women were exclusively gay.

Some of those women formed their own group. In 1955, Del Martin and Phyllis Lyon started the Daughters of Bilitis in San Francisco. (According to legend, Bilitis was an ancient Greek lesbian poet.) It was most likely America's first formal lesbian organization.

Most doctors and mental-health groups, such as the American Psychiatric Association, called homosexuality a mental illness. Then psychologist Evelyn Hooker gave psychological tests to both homosexuals and heterosexuals. In 1956, she announced that both groups were equally sane. The announcement didn't matter at first; so ingrained was the bias against gays that years would pass before Hooker's announcement had much effect.

In 1957, Frank Kameny—an astronomer working for the U.S. Army—got fired when bosses found out that he was gay. Kameny sued. He lost, but as the first federal employee to stand up against the government, he blazed a trail that many others would follow.

Gay sex was still against the law, but even that situation began to change. In 1961, Illinois became the first state to legalize gay relationships among adults, although they still faced discrimination on the job and elsewhere.

Instead of staying in hiding, more and more gays came "out of the closet," declared that they were gay, and (like members of other groups in the 1960s), organized marches and other demonstrations to demand equal rights. These events were sparks that became a giant torch on the night of June 27, 1969.

New York's Greenwich Village still housed gay bars. The police sometimes raided the bars and arrested the customers for indecent behavior. But on June 27, the men and women of the Stonewall Inn fought back.

The Stonewall riot began when police raided the bar and arrested its patrons, which at that time was a common form of harassment against establishments frequented by gays and lesbians. People both in the bar and outside on the street resisted, and threw bottles, rocks and trash at the cops. Beatings and fires followed, turning the conflict into an all-out riot that continued over the next two nights.

If Hooker, Kameny, the Mattachines, and the Daughters of Bilitis encouraged gays and lesbians to speak up for themselves, the Stonewall incident inspired them to fight. New gay organizations sprang up. "Gay pride" parades drew thousands of marchers.

The straight world noticed. "It is hereby declared to be contrary to the public policy of the City of East Lansing for any person to deny any other person the enjoyment of his/her civil rights or . . . to discriminate against any other person . . . or to harass any person because of . . . sexual orientation." So East Lansing, Michigan, announced in 1972. In so doing, East Lansing became the first American city to forbid discrimination against gays.

In 1973, the American Psychiatric Association finally heeded Evelyn Hooker and declared that homosexuality was not a sickness. During the mid-1970s, members of the House of Representatives started proposing laws for gay rights. The laws did not pass. In 1975, the U.S. Civil Service Commission changed its policies and let gays serve openly in government jobs.

The military, however, still banned gays.

Air Force Technical Sergeant Leonard Matlovich, an eleven-year combat veteran, had won a Bronze Star for distinguished service and a Purple Heart for getting wounded in combat. This war hero was hiding a secret.

On March 6, 1975, he had had enough of hiding. he wrote to the Secretary of the Air Force, "I consider myself to be a homosexual and fully qualified for further military service."

As the first serviceman in uniform to fight the military's antigay policy, Matlovich became famous. He wanted the service to throw out its ban on gay servicemen. Instead, the Air Force threw him out with a dishonorable discharge.

His dismissal was a sign of times to come.

Anita Bryant was a former finalist in the Miss America pageant, a spokeswoman for Florida orange juice, a singer, and a Christian conservative. Florida's Dade County had passed a law blocking discrimination against gays. Bryant led a crusade to overturn the law. In 1977, she won. Other communities followed, overturning their own gay-rights laws or blocking the passage of new ones.

In 1982, policemen entered the home of Georgia resident Michael Hardwick, found him in bed with another man, and arrested him for breaking the law. Georgia had a law against homosexual behavior. Hardwick faced from one to twenty years in prison.

Gays in the U.S. armed forces continue to suffer the effects of homophobia, and the current military policy of Don't Ask, Don't Tell doesn't help.

Hardwick's lawyer would have none of that. He argued that the police had invaded Hardwick's privacy and that the law was unconstitutional. Georgia's top law-enforcement official, Attorney General Michael Bowers, said the law was indeed constitutional. He asked the Supreme Court to back him up, and it did.

In *Bowers v. Hardwick* (1986), the Supreme Court invoked traditions of law, public opinion ("until 1961, all 50 states outlawed sodomy," wrote Justice Byron White), and religion ("the law," he wrote, "is constantly based on notions of morality"). In short, wrote Justice White, "[Hardwick] would have us announce . . . a fundamental right to engage in homosexual sodomy. This we are quite unwilling to do."

The Supreme Court used dignified words, but others weren't so restrained.

"The first national study of violence against gays and lesbians was made in 1984," wrote civil-rights journalist Marilyn Tower Oliver in her book *Gay and Lesbian Rights: A Struggle*. "Ninety-four percent reported being spat upon, chased, hit, or assaulted with a weapon." "Homosexuals were four times more likely to be victims of violence than persons in the general population," reported minority-rights expert Jim Carnes in *Us and Them: A History of Intolerance in America*. "A 1987 study by the U.S. Department of Justice showed gays to be the 'most frequent victims' of hate crimes," wrote author Judith C. Galas in her book *Gay Rights*. "Anti-gay violence and victimization rose 31 percent in 1991," stated Oliver.

In defense, militant organizations like ACT UP (AIDS Coalition to Unleash Power, formed in 1987) stormed the streets in angry marches and demonstrations. On a more peaceful front, many communities continued to pass laws banning discrimination against gays. In running for president in 1992, Arkansas governor Bill Clinton promised to eliminate the ban on gays in the military, and he won the election.

Colorado's Amendment 2

"Neither the state of Colorado . . . nor any of its agencies . . . shall enact, adopt, or enforce any statute . . . whereby homosexual, lesbian, or bisexual orientation, conduct, practice, or relationships shall . . . entitle any person or class of persons to have or claim any minority status, quota preferences, protected status, or claim of discrimination." That was Amendment 2, which the people of Colorado voted in 1992 to add to their state's constitution. Under Amendment 2, landlords could refuse to rent to gays, and employers could refuse to hire them.

In *Romer v. Evans* (1996), the Supreme Court struck down Amendment 2. "It identifies persons by a single trait and then denies them protection across the board," wrote Justice Anthony Kennedy. "It is not within our constitutional tradition to enact laws of this sort." He added, "Amendment 2 . . . inflicts on [gays] immediate, continuing, and real injuries . . . [and] classifies homosexuals not to further a proper legislative end but to make them unequal to everyone else. This Colorado cannot do."

The military's highest-ranking officer, chairman of the Joint Chiefs of Staff Colin Powell (who rose to the cabinet position of Secretary of State under President, George W. Bush), spoke out publicly against his then commander-in-chief's plan. So did other military officers, civilian staff members in the Defense Department, and members of the House and Senate.

Clinton compromised. "Applicants for military service will not be asked or required to reveal their sexual orientation," ordered Secretary of Defense Les Aspin in 1993. However, Aspin went on, "Service members will be separated [from military service] for homosexual conduct."

The policy was called, Don't Ask, Don't Tell. An officer couldn't ask his men if they were gay, and they didn't have to volunteer the information—but if they did, or if someone caught them in homosexual acts, the armed forces had to throw them out.

That's what the army did to Colonel Margarethe Cammermeyer, chief nurse of the Washington State National Guard and winner of a Bronze Star and a Meritorious Service medal. In the late 1980s, she was a candidate for chief nurse of the U.S. National Guard. During an interview for the job, she was asked if she was gay—the interview took place before Don't Ask, Don't Tell—and she said yes.

The army kicked her out. Cammermeyer sued. In a heavily publicized 1994 decision, U.S. District Judge Thomas Zilly ruled for Cammermeyer, although Don't Ask, Don't Tell remained in place.

As the 1990s progressed, a new cause arose: gay marriage. In 1993, Hawaii lesbian Ninia Baehr applied for a marriage license for herself and her girlfriend. When the state turned her down, she and other gay couples sued. The state Supreme Court said that if the government wanted to block gay marriages, it had to show a "compelling public interest"—that is, an overriding reason why gay marriage should be illegal. It was the first time that such a high court allowed the possibility of gay marriage.

"Full faith and credit shall be given in each state to the public acts, records, and judicial proceedings of every other state," reads the Constitution's Article IV. "The citizens of each state shall be entitled to all privileges and immunities of citizens in the [other] states." If Hawaii legalized gay marriage, any American gay couple could go to Hawaii, get married,

Despite her many achievements in military service to the United States, Colonel Margarethe Cammermeyer was kicked out of the army for being gay.

and return home legally wed, even if their home state didn't allow gay marriage.

Conservatives were frightened and furious. They fought back with the Defense of Marriage Act (1996), an end run around Article IV. "No state . . . shall be required to give effect to any public act, record, or judicial proceeding of any other state . . . respecting a relationship between persons of the same sex that is treated as a marriage . . . 'Marriage' means only a legal union between one man and one woman as husband and wife."

In December 1999, the Vermont Supreme Court weighed in. It ruled that the state must give gay couples the same protections as straight couples. No other state Supreme Court, even the one in Hawaii, had gone so far.

Four months later, Vermont's legislature legalized a "civil union" for gays, which took effect in July 2000. It was marriage in all but name.

The fight for gay marriage goes on, as do other struggles over gay rights. In 2000, for instance, the Supreme Court ruled that the Boy Scouts of America could exclude gay scoutmasters. Using that decision, other organizations can keep gays out, too.

Another ongoing fight involves gay bashing. In 1998, two men met college student Matthew Shepard in a gay bar in Laramie, Wyoming. All three went outside, where the two young men beat Shepard, tied him to a fence, and left him there to die, simply because they didn't like gays. The incident caused nationwide protests against violence done to gays, but violence continues to break out.

No doubt there will be other struggles, not to mention problems that no one today can foresee. There will always be Anita Bryants to denounce gay rights—and people like the Stonewall Inn customers to fight back.

7 Where We Go Now

Everyone has rights. In recent decades, almost everyone has been claiming them.

People with Disabilities

More than 40 million Americans have eyes, ears, brains, or limbs that don't work properly. Decades ago, they would have had few places to get help, except for some charities and a few organizations that benefit disabled people.

Things started to change in the last half of the twentieth century. In 1968, Congress passed the Architectural Barriers Act, which forced all federal buildings to provide ramps and other means of easy access for people who couldn't walk well.

The Rehabilitation Act of 1973 went further. "No otherwise qualified individual with handicaps," read the Act, "shall solely by reason of his/her handicap . . . be subjected to discrimination under any program or activity receiving federal financial assistance."

In 1975, Congress roped schools into the story with the Education for All Handicapped Children Act and the Individuals with Disabilities Education Act. The laws ordered schools to set up special courses and other programs for disabled students.

The most important law yet to benefit the disabled, the Americans with Disabilities Act (ADA), was passed in 1990. The ADA sought "the elimination of discrimination against individuals with disabilities . . . [and] clear, strong, consistent, enforceable standards addressing discrimination against individuals with disabilities." The act addressed everything from ramps for wheelchairs to lawsuits against employers who discriminate.

Ten years after the act became law, the disabled still had a long way to go to achieve equality with nondisabled citizens. A survey by the Louis Harris polling organization found that "only 32 percent of people with disabilities said they currently hold full- or part-time jobs, compared to 81 percent of those without disabilities." The reason, according to the Cornell University School of Industrial and Labor Relations, was "the negative attitudes of supervisors and co-workers toward disabled people."

The disabled fought those attitudes both on the job and in the halls of government. Disabled students filed about 30,000 complaints with the Department of Education's Office for Civil Rights. Meanwhile, disabled workers filed more than 125,000 complaints with the U.S. Equal Opportunity Commission, which oversees ADA cases. No doubt the disabled will continue to fight. After all, can more than 40 million Americans be wrong?

Children and Teenagers

For much of American history, children had no rights. By law, they were more or less the property of their fathers. A father could lease out his children to long, hard labor in factories or fields, take their wages, and beat them for disobeying him or for no reason at all.

For disobeying the government, a child might get slightly lighter treatment. The Massachusetts Body of Liberties, for instance, gave "children, idiots, distracted persons, and all that are strangers or newcomers" a little more leeway than the strict, hard-line justice that it imposed on adults. Life for minors stayed under such laws for a long time, in Massachusetts and elsewhere.

Things began to change in the wave of reforms that swept over the country during the first half of the 1800s. In the late 1830s and early 1840s, Massachusetts and Connecticut slightly limited the hours and days that a child could work.

But large-scale change in the laws as they protect children in the United States didn't arrive until 1899. Until then, children who committed crimes were tried like adults and imprisoned along with them. But in 1899, Illinois passed the Juvenile Court Act, "which established the nation's first juvenile court and gave rise to new procedures for dealing with child lawbreakers," according to Ann Gaines in her book *Prisons*. "The stated goal of the juvenile system was always to do what was best for the child; treatment, not punishment." Within twenty years, almost every state had its own juvenile justice system.

Law-abiding children faced a mixed bag. Not until the late 1930s and early 1940s did the Congress, the president, and the Supreme Court approve laws that regulated working conditions and hours for Americans under age sixteen.

Around the same time, children got freedom of religion. In *West Virginia Board of Education v. Barnette* (1943), the Supreme Court decided that children of a Jehovah's Witness family didn't have to salute the American flag in school. (Witness doctrine says that saluting the flag violates the Bible's Third Commandment, "Thou shalt not worship a graven image.") *Engel v. Vitale* (1962) established that schools could not force children to pray in class.

Crime committed by children remained a sticky issue, though. If the police arrested an adult, he had the right to get a lawyer, question witnesses, and have a fair trial. A teenager had no such rights. The Supreme Court gave them to minors with *In Re Gault* (1967).

The Court widened a child's right to express himself or herself, too. In *Tinker v. Des Moines Independent School District* (1969), the Court ruled that the school district had no right to punish a student who wore a black armband to protest the Vietnam War.

The fight for minors' rights peaked two years later. For decades, Americans became legal adults—able to vote and exercise other rights—at age twenty-one. Men as young as eighteen had long been fighting and dying in Vietnam, however. If a person was old enough to die for his or her country, the feeling went, he or she was old enough to vote in its elections. In 1971, the Twenty-Sixth Amendment lowered the voting age to eighteen.

Nevertheless, minors didn't have every right that adults did. In *Ginsberg v. New York* (1968), the Supreme Court ruled that a news dealer could sell obscene magazines to adults but not to kids. *Wisconsin v. Yoder* (1972) saw the Court rule that parents control their children's education and could pull them out of school for years, even if the local government and the kids themselves objected.

When it came to children who did go to school, the Court strengthened the schools' power. In *New Jersey v. TLO* (1985), the Court ruled that high-school students didn't have as wide a right to privacy as adults. With *Bethel School District No. 403 v. Fraser* (1986), the Court let schools cut off a student's freedom of expression if he made speeches about sex. In *Hazelwood School District v. Kuhlmeier* (1988), the Court added that schools could censor student publications.

The Supreme Court wasn't the only entity to limit the rights of kids. Young criminals frightened many adults, who pressured their government to get kids off the streets. By the late 1990s, about three-quarters of all American cities had installed curfews to force minors indoors late at night. At the same time, a rising number of juvenile criminals were being tried in adult courts and sent to adult prisons.

"Teenagers are being interrogated, suspended, reprimanded, and even arrested—not for committing actual crimes but for what they say in class, write on tests, post on the Internet, or e-mail to a friend, as well as what they wear, and even how they do their hair," *New York Times* journalist Ethan Bronner summed up in late 1999. "Taken together, civil-liberties advocates say, these policies amount to the biggest crackdown on teen rights in recent history."

In many areas of rights and rules, cracking down eventually leads to loosening up. No one knows when—or if—the rules will loosen for children and teenagers.

Senior Citizens

If being under eighteen means being under restrictions, so does being over the age of sixty-five—or even over forty.

Age discrimination wasn't an issue in America's early years, because most people didn't reach old age. For every exception like Benjamin Franklin, who lived to be eighty-four, thousands of others died young. War, childbirth, accidents, and disease took so many young people that the life expectancy for Americans in 1776 was less than forty years. Even by 1900, it was under fifty years.

But in the 1960s, millions were living into their sixties and seventies. Younger people didn't seem to be comfortable with these older adults. Many companies set mandatory retirement schedules. If you were sixty-five, the company kicked you out, even if you could still do your job. If you applied for a new job, you would likely see companies turn you down because of your age—even if you were fifty-five or even forty-five.

Congress' Age Discrimination in Employment Act of 1967 tried to stop all that. Aimed at workers age forty and over, the law told employers that they couldn't fire a worker or turn down an applicant for a job just because he was getting up in years. Eight years later, the Age Discrimination Act of 1975 extended these protections from employers to any organization that got money from the federal government.

Laws like these encouraged older people to fight for themselves. In 1981, for example, more than 11,000 people lodged age-discrimination complaints with the federal government's Equal Employment Opportunity Commission.

Even more cases and complaints may be on the way. In a 1999 issue of the business magazine *Training*, editor Ron Zemke noted "today's up-front hostility and contempt aimed at older workers." He explained, "Underlying such ire is the simple fact that 78 million baby boomers [people born between 1946 and 1964] are standing between every [young] Generation Xer" and a top job. The financial magazine *Fortune* has predicted that by the end of 2003, "there will be more workers over forty than there are workers under forty."

They may have a hard time. In 2000, the middle-aged and elderly suffered a loss when, in *Kimel v. Florida Board of Regents,* the Supreme Court said that state governments didn't have to obey the Age Discrimination in Employment Act.

Fights for jobs can get very nasty. For the future, expect plenty of harsh words—lots of them in lawsuits.

Animal Rights

Most early Americans couldn't have imagined what animal rights meant. The term didn't exist.

The early colonists valued animals highly, of course. Farmers couldn't plow without horses or mules. Cows and sheep supplied both food and fabric. Dogs were loyal friends when life got lonely and sharp-fanged protectors when it got dangerous. Said the Massachusetts Body of

Liberties, "No man shall exercise any tyranny or cruelty towards any brute creatures which are usually kept for man's use."

Animals were property like land or houses, and had no legal rights. Things shifted in the animals' direction in the late 1890s. More and more Americans moved off farms and into cities, or were born there. They began to see animals as something more than tools to use on the job. A good number of them joined animal-protection groups like the American Society for the Prevention of Cruelty to Animals.

Meanwhile, science had found a new use for animals. Some beasts' bodies are similar to human bodies, and doctors cut animals open to study anatomy and tested medicines on them.

By the 1950s, quite a few people objected to using animals in the lab. Some citizens called on doctors to keep the animals from suffering more than necessary and to reduce the number of animals that they used.

Even Congress got involved. The Animal Welfare Act of 1966 "requires scientists to provide adequate care for laboratory animals," wrote *Science World* magazine journalist Maria L. Chang.

At the same time, humanity was destroying entire species. The spread of people and pollution killed thousands of creatures.

To protect them, Congress passed the Endangered Species Act of 1973. It allowed the government to set aside certain animals as members of protected species. Killing them would be against the law.

These cages housed dogs, monkeys, sheep, and donkeys used for testing biological toxins in Iraq. Many countries dismiss the pain and suffering of animals used in scientific experiments.

The real beginning of the modern animal-rights movement came in 1975 with the book *Animal Liberation* by Australian activist Peter Singer. He felt that people should respect any creatures who can perceive the world around them and react to it.

Animal Liberation launched a wave of animal-rights demands. If a creature can suffer, said some activists, then it has the right not to suffer. Others said that if a creature has emotions, memories, and a personality, it should have more or less the same rights as anyone else with emotions, memories, and a personality, including humans.

Some activists have done more than just talk. "The Association of American Medical Colleges has recorded almost 4,000 cases of intimidation [of medical researchers] by animal-rights activists," reported *The Economist* magazine in 1991. "One raid, at a campus of the University of California in 1987, caused 3.5 million dollars' worth of damage to a veterinary center."

The use of lab animals dropped. Communities around the country toughened their laws against cruelty toward animals. In 1999, the prestigious Harvard Law School announced that it would present its first course in animal law.

"How animals are treated has become an important issue in international relations," *Christian Science Monitor* correspondent Brad Knickerbocker wrote at the end of 1999. "Activists are pushing for what would amount to a radically different status for animals—more nearly like humans in terms of civil rights."

Conclusion

Civil rights are like the country itself: alive, changing, and sometimes producing very complex situations. In the Declaration of Independence, Thomas Jefferson listed the most important rights simply.

"We hold these truths to be self-evident: that all men are created equal, that they are endowed by their creator with certain unalienable rights, that among these are life, liberty, and the pursuit of happiness."

Preamble to the Constitution

We the People of the United States, in order to form a more perfect Union, establish Justice, insure domestic Tranquility, provide for the common defence, promote the general Welfare, and secure the Blessings of Liberty to ourselves and our Posterity, do ordain and establish this Constitution for the United States of America.

On September 25, 1789, Congress transmitted to the state legislatures twelve proposed amendments, two of which, having to do with congressional representation and congressional pay, were not adopted. The remaining ten amendments became the Bill of Rights.

The Bill of Rights

Amendment I

Congress shall make no law respecting an establishment of religion, or prohibiting the free exercise thereof; or abridging the freedom of speech, or of the press; or the right of the people peaceably to assemble, and to petition the Government for a redress of grievances.

Amendment II

A well regulated Militia, being necessary to the security of a free State, the right of the people to keep and bear Arms, shall not be infringed.

Amendment III

No Soldier shall, in time of peace be quartered in any house, without the consent of the Owner, nor in time of war, but in a manner to be prescribed by law.

Amendment IV

The right of the people to be secure in their persons, houses, papers, and effects, against unreasonable searches and seizures, shall not be violated, and no Warrants shall issue, but upon probable cause, supported by Oath or affirmation, and particularly describing the place to be searched, and the persons or things to be seized.

Amendment V

No person shall be held to answer for a capital, or otherwise infamous crime, unless on a presentment or indictment of a Grand Jury, except in cases arising in the land or naval forces, or in the Militia, when in actual service in time of War or public danger; nor shall any person be subject for the same offence to be twice put in jeopardy of life or limb; nor shall be compelled in any criminal case to be a witness against himself, nor be deprived of life, liberty, or property, without due process of law; nor shall private property be taken for public use, without just compensation.

Amendment VI

In all criminal prosecutions, the accused shall enjoy the right to a speedy and public trial, by an impartial jury of the State and district wherein the crime shall have been committed, which district shall have been previously ascertained by law, and to be informed of the nature and cause of the accusation; to be confronted with the witnesses against him; to have compulsory process for obtaining witnesses in his favor, and to have the Assistance of Counsel for his defence.

Amendment VII

In Suits at common law, where the value in controversy shall exceed twenty dollars, the right of trial by jury shall be preserved, and no fact tried by a jury, shall be otherwise re-examined in any Court of the United States, than according to the rules of the common law.

Amendment VIII

Excessive bail shall not be required, nor excessive fines imposed, nor cruel and unusual punishments inflicted.

Amendment IX

The enumeration in the Constitution, of certain rights, shall not be construed to deny or disparage others retained by the people.

Amendment X

The powers not delegated to the United States by the Constitution, nor prohibited by it to the States, are reserved to the States respectively, or to the people.

Timeline

About 1800 BC
King Hammurabi of Babylon creates the Code of Hammurabi, the oldest surviving list of laws.

1215
King John of England signs the Magna Carta. The document defines the just treatment of various classes.

1512
Father Bartholome de las Casas wages the first known campaign for Indian rights.

1619
In Jamestown, Virginia, African slaves are delivered to America for the first time.

1641
English settlers establish the Massachusetts Body of Liberties, which ensures the rights of citizens.

1689

The English Bill of Rights grants the people a range of freedoms and powers.

1776

American politician Thomas Jefferson writes the Declaration of Independence, in which American colonists declare themselves free of British rule.

1787

The U.S. Congress passes the Northwest Ordinance, the first major national law dealing with Indians. It also outlaws slavery in some areas.

1787

American politicians, particularly James Madison, write the U.S. Constitution.

1791

The Bill of Rights is added to the Constitution, establishing additional rights and freedoms.

1830

Congress passes the Indian Removal Act to move the Indians off their lands.

1857

In the case of *Dred Scott v. Sandford*, the U.S. Supreme Court decides that slaves can't be freed by going to states where Congress has outlawed slavery. The decision will help to bring on the Civil War.

1863

President Lincoln signs the Emancipation Proclamation, which outlaws slavery.

1868

Congress passes the Fourteenth Amendment to the Constitution. The amendment grants all citizens equal protection of the nation's laws.

1869

Elizabeth Cady Stanton and Susan B. Anthony form the National Woman Suffrage Association to campaign for women to have the right to vote.

1871

Congress passes the Civil Rights Act of 1871, under which citizens can sue anyone who deprives them of their rights.

1882

Congress passes the Immigration Act and the Chinese Exclusion Act to control immigration.

1883

In *Ex Parte Crow Dog*, the Supreme Court rules that Indians can regulate their own internal affairs.

1887

Congress passes the General Allotment Act, also called the Dawes Act, which deprives the Indians of most of their land.

1896

In *Plessy v. Ferguson*, the Supreme Court approves the "separate but equal" doctrine and enables local governments to segregate blacks from whites.

1920

The United States ratifies the Nineteenth Amendment to the Constitution, which gives women the right to vote.

1924

Congress passes the Indian Citizenship Act, which makes Native Americans full citizens of the United States.

1924

Congress passes the Immigration Act, which drastically cuts the number of immigrants.

1934

Congress passes the Indian Reorganization Act, which decrees Native American self-government.

1948

President Harry Truman orders the military to integrate all races in the services.

1950

Harry Hay and others form the Mattachine Society, the first modern American gay organization.

1954

In *Brown v. Board of Education of Topeka, Kansas*, the Supreme Court overturns *Plessy v. Ferguson* and outlaws the doctrine of "separate but equal."

1955

Black seamstress Rosa Parks of Montgomery, Alabama, refuses to give up her seat on a bus to a white man and is arrested. The incident leads to the Montgomery bus boycott, the first large-scale act of the modern black civil rights movement.

1957

Arkansas governor Orval Faubus refuses to let black students enter Little Rock Central High School, and sparks a national controversy over civil rights.

1963

More than 200,000 Americans march on Washington, DC, to demonstrate against racial segregation. At the event, the Rev. Dr. Martin Luther King Jr. recites his "I Have a Dream" speech, which becomes an inspiration and rallying point.

1964

Congress passes the Civil Rights Act, which outlaws discrimination on the basis of color, race, religion, national origin, or gender.

1965

Congress passes the Voting Rights Act, which outlaws literacy tests and other obstacles to black voting.

1965

Congress passes the Immigration Act, which allows massive waves of immigrants into America.

1967

Congress passes the Age Discrimination in Employment Act, which forces employers to ignore a worker's age in hiring and firing.

1969

A police raid on the Stonewall Inn, a New York gay bar, sparks uprisings for gay rights.

1973

In *Roe v. Wade*, the Supreme Court gives women the right to have an abortion.

1973

Congress passes the Endangered Species Act to protect rare animals.

1980

Congress passes the Civil Rights of Institutionalized Persons Act to protect prisoners from "grievous harm."

1986

In *Bowers v. Hardwick*, the Supreme Court rules that states can outlaw homosexual acts.

1988

Congress passes the Indian Gaming Regulatory Act, allowing Native Americans to establish casinos.

1990

Congress passes the Americans with Disabilities Act, which outlaws discrimination against disabled people.

1993

Secretary of Defense Les Aspin decrees a Don't Ask, Don't Tell policy regarding gay men and women in military service.

Glossary

AIM   The American Indian Movement, formed in 1968 to speak out for Native American rights.

Americans with Disabilities Act   A law guaranteeing equal rights for those with disabilities. Signed into law in 1990.

animal rights   The idea that animals deserve the rights of human beings.

Animal Welfare Act   A law passed by Congress in 1966 to guarantee humane treatment for laboratory animals.

civil rights   The concept of equality for all people.

Declaration of Independence   Written by Thomas Jefferson and signed in 1776, it laid down the basic principles of American government.

Dred Scott vs. Sandford **(Dred Scott Case)**   The first civil rights case in America, tried in 1857. Scott's bid for freedom was turned down by the U.S. Supreme Court.

freedom riders   Northern Civil Rights advocates in the late 1950s and the 1960s who rode buses to the south to protest segregation.

gay rights   Equal rights for homosexuals.

immigrant   Someone from another country than his or her country of residence.

Juvenile Court Act   Passed in Illinois in 1899, this set up the first Juvenile Court so that children need not be tried as or with adults.

Magna Carta   The first English bill of rights, signed by King John in 1215.

NAACP   National Association for the Advancement of Colored People, an organization for African American rights, founded in 1909.

NOW   The National Organization for Women, an equal rights organization founded in1966.

prisoners' rights   The idea of humane treatment of prisoners.

women's suffrage   The right of women to vote.

For More Information

Organizations

American Civil Liberties Union
125 Broad Street
New York, NY 10004
(212) 344-3005
Web site: http://www.aclu.org

Amnesty International
322 Eighth Avenue
New York, NY 10001
(212) 807-8400
or
600 Pennsylvania Avenue Southeast
Washington, DC 20003
(202) 544-0200
Web site: http://www.amnesty.org

The Freedom Forum
1101 Wilson Boulevard
Arlington, VA 22209
(703) 528-0800
Web site: http://www.freedomforum.org

Freedom House
1319 18th Street NW
Washington, DC 20036
(202) 296-5101
Web site: http://www.freedomhouse.org

Human Rights Watch
350 Fifth Avenue, 34th Floor
New York, NY 10118
(212) 290-4700
Web site: http://www.hrw.org

Leadership Conference on Civil Rights
1629 K Street NW
Washington, DC 20006
(202) 466-3311
Web site: http://www.civilrights.org/lccr

United States Commission on Civil Rights
624 9th Street NW
Washington, DC 20425
(202) 376-8312
Web site: http://www.usccr.gov

United States Department of Justice
Civil Rights Division
P.O. Box 65808
Washington, DC 20035
(202) 514-4609
Web site: http://www.usdoj.gov/crt/crt-home.html

Web Sites

Civilrights.org
http://www.civilrights.org

FindLaw.com
http://www.findlaw.com/01topics/36civil

Human Rights Web
http://www.hrweb.org

IGC Internet Progressive Gateway
http://www.igc.org

The Oyez Project
http://www.oyez.com

The Steward for Human and Civil Rights
http://www.thesteward.net

For Further Reading

Amar, Akhil Reed, and Alan Hirsch. *For The People: What the Constitution Really Says About Your Rights.* New York: The Free Press, 1998.

Carnes, Jim. *Us and Them: A History of Intolerance in America.* New York: Oxford University Press, 1996.

Carruth, Gorton. *What Happened When: A Chronology of Life & Events in America.* New York: Signet, 1991.

Foner, Eric. *The Story of American Freedom.* New York: Norton, 1998.

Forer, Lois G. *Unequal Protection: Women, Children and the Elderly in Court.* New York: Norton, 1991.

Hentoff, Nat. *Living the Bill of Rights: How to Be an Authentic American.* New York: HarperCollins, 1998.

Levy, Debbie. *Civil Liberties.* San Diego, CA: Lucent Books, 2000.

Nardo, Don. *The Bill of Rights.* San Diego, CA: Greenhaven Press, 1998.

Palmer, Kris E. *Constitutional Amendments: 1789 to the Present.* Detroit: Gale Group, 2000.

Peck, Rodney G. *Working Together Against Human Rights Violations.* New York: Rosen Publishing Group, 1995.

Ravitch, Diane and Abigail Thernstrom, eds. *The Democracy Reader: Classic and Modern Speeches, Essays, Poems, Declarations, and Documents on Freedom and Human Rights Worldwide.* New York: HarperCollins, 1992.

Roleff, Tamara L., ed. *Civil Liberties: Opposing Viewpoints.* San Diego, CA: Greenhaven, 1999.

Spence, Gerry. *Give Me Liberty!: Freeing Ourselves in the Twenty-First Century.* New York: St. Martin's Press, 1998.

Walker, Samuel. *The Rights Revolution: Rights and Community in Modern America.* New York: Oxford University Press, 1998.

Williams, Mary E., ed. *Human Rights: Opposing Viewpoints.* San Diego, CA: Greenhaven, 1998.

Index

About the Author

David Seidman is a professional writer who has published many books, including *All Gone: Things That Aren't There Anymore*, *Exploring Careers in Journalism*, and *The Young Zillionaire's Guide to Supply and Demand*. He lives in California.

Acknowledgments

As always, thanks to my attorney, Paul Levine, for helping to make the business arrangements that enabled me to write this book. Thanks also to the libraries of the city of Los Angeles, the county of Los Angeles, the University of California Los Angeles, and especially the city of Beverly Hills for research assistance.

Photo Credits

DATE DUE

APR 2 5 2002
APR 2 5 2002

GAYLORD

PRINTED IN U.S.A.